THE CABBIE'S TALE

TIM FASANO

THE CABBIE'S TALE

A MEMOIR

Coyote Canyon Press
Claremont, California

COYOTE CANYON PRESS

All rights reserved. No part of this book may be reproduced in any form or by any electronic or mechanical means, including information storage and retrieval systems, without permission in writing from the publisher, except in the case of short passages quoted in reviews.

Published by Coyote Canyon Press, Claremont, California in 2020.

Copyright © 2020 by Coyote Canyon Press
ISBN 978-1-7321903-6-8
Cover art by Dmitry Samarov

www.coyotecanyonpress.com

Editor's Note: Almost all the writing in this book comes from Tim Fasano's original blog, *Tampa Taxi Shots* (timfasano.typepad.com). The organizing principle of this book was to condense five years of blog entries into a single year. For the most part, the events recounted took place in 2009 although some may have occurred one or two years before or after. Most names of people have been changed as well as names of cab companies and government agencies.

JANUARY

JANUARY 1

New Year's Eve rocks. For the first time in months, I made some real money, driving over 260 miles, roughly the distance to Miami, all of it racked up in the Tampa Bay area. It's too bad every night isn't like this — although I could've done without the rain, which came down in torrential sheets, flooding the roads fast but at least waiting until after the ball dropped.

I got paid in cash on all fares, which is good because I don't accept credit cards or checks. One woman did slide her checkbook out of her purse; and when I told her I don't accept checks, she kept saying *look at my big house* like it was collateral. She eventually got the money from her babysitter, making me wonder how she was going to pay her back. The problem is simple: payments by credit card or check go straight into the company's pocket. I don't see a penny of it until the lease is paid.

After the bars closed, I had several rides to Mons Venus and 2001 Odyssey, famous strip clubs, both of which are open until five in the morning. When I pulled in around 3:30 A.M., half the limos in Tampa were there and about thirty cabs. Everyone appeared to be on their cell phones.

I did get some trips over the bay when I gave accurate estimates. A couple I took to Clearwater said the "scab cab" wanted $80 apiece. I estimated $55, and they gave me a huge tip.

On the way home, right before sunup, I pulled into a 7-Eleven and saw two women fighting in the parking lot. One had fallen to her knees, shirt ripped, exposing her bra. The other woman was pulling her hair and hitting her furiously on the back of the head with closed fists. I could hear the first woman's shrieks and cries, like those of a wounded animal, as a circle of men gathered.

Happy New Year!

JANUARY 2

I'm a cab driver. That's an honest profession. It's a profession that requires about 60–70 hours a week from me, and it's hard work. It's not easy work. You get cussed at, yelled at. Half the time you don't pick up people under favorable conditions. They're calling for a taxicab because something has gone wrong in their lives. And you hear it. It's a tough job.

Cab drivers are independent contractors and don't earn a salary or hourly wage. We pay the company for the right to work. We lease our cabs and pay for our gas. What's left is ours. In short, we work on straight commission. Running my own little business can be a bit rough sometimes. The logistics don't always go my way, but I like that the company can't control my activities.

A driver's income can be sporadic, which makes it hard to look at a calendar and plan. The buck might not be there. However, there are times like now when business is brisk. Too bad it's not brisk year-round.

I work many hours, sometimes seventy hours a week, and I rarely take a day off. Many drivers work these kinds of hours, mostly out of necessity, putting in about fifteen a day for little money.

My gas and lease are high, so much so that rolling on a call whose destination is only a couple miles away isn't worth my time.

Short drives are frustrating, and so is listening to people accusing me of long-routing them. Most drivers have a GPS device they paid for themselves. The company doesn't provide these. GPS tells us precisely how to get to our destination. Drivers would never spend the money just to jerk customers around. Why would they do that?

JANUARY 3

On New Year's Day, I-275 was backed up in all directions because of the Outback Bowl and an accident going into the airport. Some guy lost control of his car on the slick road and crashed into the guard rail.

I arrived on the scene right after it happened and couldn't avoid the delay. As I was letting the ambulance in, a yellow cab pulled in behind it. The driver must've been thinking this was his ticket around the mess; but with traffic stopped in both directions, nobody was going anywhere. My fare, a businessman in an expensive suit, missed his flight. He wasn't happy.

When I got home that night, Kate phoned. She was my girlfriend for a short period of time five years ago until her life fell apart, and she split for reasons beyond anyone's ability to help or comprehend; but apparently she inherited a modest sum of money and moved back to Florida and was living in her mother's condo near Bayonet Point, close to Hudson. I accepted her invitation to visit, but I'd never heard of Bayonet Point and had to look it up.

We ate pizza and watched movies, including *Spartacus*. Charles Laughton and his nemesis Laurence Olivier are phenomenal as a Roman General and Senator at odds with each other. I especially love Peter Ustinov's line: "Add courage to your newfound virtues."

We hung out, and I was able to relax for the first time in a while. It was hard to believe I hadn't seen her for so long, but by the end of my stay, she was knee-walking drunk and getting very angry. So I left, regrettably, but it was the right decision.

JANUARY 4

My friend and fellow cabbie, Tammy, likes to take holidays off and go to the Blue Ridge Mountains of North Carolina, where she hopes to retire one day. I'm happy for people who can plan their lives so far ahead. Tammy's worked hard for her future happiness, but recently I heard she was sick and was taking some time off.

Taking time off is essential to one's health. Several of my friends have died under the stress and uncertainty of these times. I know when you get to be my age, you say goodbye to people and things. I guess that's a normal part of aging, but recently things have been especially difficult.

JANUARY 5

There's this guy from New York who writes a taxi blog called *Return Cabbie*. He tried to look me up when he was in Tampa recently. Unfortunately, it was when my Internet was down, and my e-mail was kaput, so I didn't know he was in town until today when I read his blog post.

A few hours before his return flight to La Guardia, he made it to Gulf Beach Transportation (one of the largest public transportation companies on the West Coast of Florida). He ran into a few drivers coming in and waiting to go out. Not one knew Tim Fasano.

What's crazy is I was at the cab lot at the time. He took a photo of my van parked across the street, having no idea it was mine. (I'm one of the few Allied Cab drivers who park off the lot.) He came by in the afternoon — right at the time I'd be there too. I would've liked to meet him.

In the aforementioned blog post, he wrote about a scary experience while visiting Tampa. He was headed over the Gandy Bridge and ran into a horrendous thunder-and-lightning storm. Torrential rainfall flooded the highway, causing him to hydroplane and almost spin over the guardrail.

JANUARY 6

A local community blog has a two-part series on curbing prostitution in Tampa. Coincidentally, *The Tampa Tribune* ran an article yesterday about the changes on Kennedy Boulevard, such as new growth and a drop-off in crime.

When I started driving a cab fourteen years ago, prostitutes and crackheads were a common sight on Kennedy. Today, not even two-bit pimps are visible.

Seminole Heights blog believes community involvement, combined with police action, is the reason for this. As far as police activity in the area, I see it every day.

JANUARY 7

The sidewalk on Bayshore Boulevard has a spectacular view of downtown, which is why people enjoy walking, cycling, and jogging there. The city claims it's the world's longest continuous sidewalk at 4.5 miles. (Actually, the longest continuous sidewalk is the Rambla of Montevideo at 13.7 miles.)

Joggers and exercisers are common this time of year, unlike most of the year when it's sweltering outside. That's why I like January. I find winters in Florida enjoyable, and today I was out walking and getting in some cardio on my day off from weight training.

I could see the herringbone sky, which means frigid air moving in. That's the extent of my knowledge of meteorology.

JANUARY 8

One thing you can count on if you drive late nights is that guys will switch gears, trying for a sure thing. When they realize they're not going to get laid, they soon get very stupid.

I had a call at Bennigan's Tavern Stadium about 2 A.M. This guy from Washington was down for the game and wanted to know if I knew where a "Jack Shack" was. After fourteen years of driving a cab, I know where just about anything of that nature is in Tampa.

One concern I have for all my fares is their security and safety. I won't troll down streets looking for girls, which is way too dangerous — and illegal.

As it turned out, this guy was in the shack for only a few minutes. He decided against it, saying the chicks were too old, then admitting he was scared of losing his money. He would've spent $150 for a hand job! (I don't know that from personal experience. It's what I've been told.)

I took him back to his hotel and got $30 and didn't have to give him a hand job.

JANUARY 9

I was quoted in the *St. Petersburg Times* this morning. The article was about renewal fees for cabbies being raised to $65.

"This is an exorbitant rate increase and comes when drivers

can least afford it," they quoted from my blog. "Times are hard. Many drivers have been foreclosed on and have fallen behind on rent. Many, like myself, are barely surviving."

JANUARY 10

This time of year, I head for the airport. Tampa International is very busy between January and April. I wish that were true throughout the year.

Last week there was a notable photographers convention in Tampa. Conventioneers were flying in from all over the country. Since parts of downtown were roped off, I'd shoot up Cleveland to Howard and hit the interstate toward the airport to pick up again.

I did get a call to Tarpon Springs, which meant a long ride. The fare turned out to be an Adobe rep, and I enjoyed chatting with him about Photoshop. In the end, it was like he paid me to listen to him.

JANUARY 11

I have a phrase for the back lot of the cab company: THE CAB GRAVEYARD. Each cab can go for about three years or 300,000 miles before it ends up here. The lot is a surprisingly pleasant place, and I always enjoy strolling through it.

Today I had a short conversation with Shoe, our weekend dispatcher and one of the most helpful guys I know. He's a big animal lover, and this morning I saw him tossing bread out for the birds, little sparrows he began feeding a while back. They've formed a flock and refuse to leave the lot. Shoe gave me some bread to toss out for them, and they came flying right over and began pecking away.

I remember the first time I visited Shoe's house. I thought it was Busch Gardens. He had cats and birds and lizards and an assortment of wildlife out by the river. They were like his pets. I especially liked the turtles.

JANUARY 12

Many new drivers try to turn driving into a nine-to-five job, but they soon realize there's nothing routine about it. Many old-timers put in shift work just like they were union workers from the northeast. It's impressive to see them do this. What I figured out is that the best business is when most people are asleep. Whenever I work overnight, bar closures and 4 A.M. airport calls put money in my pocket. Unfortunately, I can't always work nights. I have daytime interests and find it hard to sleep when the sun is out.

When I work days, I try to make STAND 21 a part of my daily activities. It's the Hyde Park stand, where cab drivers go when they're waiting for a call. Many drivers think that STAND 21 is the land of milk and honey, the mythical place where cabbies will find their fortune.

Trouble is nowadays there are too many cabs parked at this stand, usually guys trying to make it a regular job. They're a nuisance, and I wish they'd learn to drive the smart way, that is, cruising around and taking calls. Today, for example, I never got near the place and made some good money.

JANUARY 13

Over the years, I've driven through Hyde Park Village countless times. I even remember when Selena's was *the* place, and outdoor jazz once a month in the village was a standing event. That's how far back I go. What I've seen countless times as well was a red phone booth. Today, I saw where it said TAXI on top.

I parked, got out of the cab, grabbed my Canon, and tried to compose some shots of it and the surrounding architecture. My understanding is that it's an old-style British phone booth, probably common in Bermuda.

While I was taking a few snapshots, a friend of mine who drives for Bay Cab pulled up to shoot the breeze.

I like Neil. He's very educated, even went to an Ivy League school, but he's a little eccentric.

Hacks spend countless hours in their cabs and often carry books, newspapers, snacks, a flashlight, a camera, the list goes on. Neil is different. *He carries a bunny rabbit with him!*

He says Fluffy is his best friend. He claims women think Fluffy is cute, and they all want to pet him, and it helps with tips. It's true when you get in a cab, the last thing you're expecting to see is a rabbit. Most drivers hate picking up animals because we get too many little old ladies at the vet's with cats in carriers just going around the corner, but I like getting those kinds of calls because I currently don't have a cat and miss my little calico, Spotty Kitty. She disappeared when they tented my old apartment. I think it scared her off. I hope that's what happened to her. I'm distraught at the idea of losing her.

JANUARY 14

I've made friends with two drivers from our international division. Allison, one of our female drivers, is from England. Sampson is from Ethiopia. The two are terrific friends and drinking buddies.

They always have cigarettes and coffee cups whenever I see them at a taxi stand. Cigarettes and coffee are a staple among drivers. I don't smoke, but I do consume massive amounts of coffee. It comes with the job.

I took advantage of a gray and misty morn to walk over to a retention pond next to STAND 21 and found some cool birds. I think one of them was a baby roseate spoonbill, a bird more often seen in south Florida. I did see one later at the cruise ship terminal where the Royal Caribbean liner was anchored. One thing I love about Florida is that I don't need an airline ticket to exotic destinations to find interesting subjects to photograph.

JANUARY 15

I drove to the airport after dropping off a fare, nothing out of the ordinary, except I had the radio on and heard a driver say, "This new system is fucked up." My customer heard it as well. Oops!

I pulled into the holding area, and several cabs followed me. I don't know why. We weren't moving. One driver said he hadn't budged in the four hours he'd been there.

The reason we're getting hosed is that the Tampa International Airport Authority has moved all cabs to the quad area, convinced that we're the cause of the traffic tie-ups at the terminal. The real reason is that the airport is one-fifth the size necessary to accommodate all the traffic. The result is that nobody is making money anymore.

This morning on Dale Mabry, I was behind an ABC cab, and he was weaving all over the place. He turned into STAND 23. I asked him why he was all over the road, and he said he was counting his money. Lucky him! He has money to count. With the sunny weather up north, Tampa is empty right now, and drivers aren't counting much money.

We can only hope that the Tampa Convention Center will be busy for the next three months. There was a convention of student musicians this week, but it was a statewide gathering. Everyone drove to Tampa and didn't need our services.

JANUARY 16

One of our drivers is the fastest runner in the world! At least he used to be. In the Montreal Olympic Games of 1976, Ian represented the Bahamas in the 100 meters and 4x100 relay. His relay team had a modicum of success, advancing to the semifinals against formidable opponents. They didn't advance to the finals.

If Ian were running today, he'd have a chance to convert his track success into a paycheck. Athletes of his era had to stop running after school to get jobs to pay the bills. Ian went to the University of Iowa and played football, but he was never able to convert his athletic talent into cash.

I met Ian years ago when he was driving a cab after going through a difficult period when he was homeless for several months. I remember giving him money for food when I could.

He remains proud of his running days and is honored to have represented his country at the Olympics.

JANUARY 17

At the corner of MacDill and Azeele, they're doing road construction. They've been fooling around with this for months, and it doesn't look any different. Almost every day, they're repositioning signs and barricades, and I never really see anyone doing anything.

As I was pulling out onto Azeele from the parking lot of the Sunoco Gas Station, I looked to the left and pulled around the brand-new NO LEFT sign, which you can't see when looking to the left.

As I approached Kennedy, I saw in the distance behind me flashing blue lights. A cop was hauling ass to catch up with me. I pulled into the Bank of America parking lot. The cop said I made an illegal left turn. Keep in mind this was Saturday morning at 7:03 when nobody was around. Well, excuse me if I didn't see the sign they threw up overnight and which hasn't been there for the last fourteen years.

He wrote me a $170 ticket. I guess I can add that to the other one I got before Christmas.

Tampa has a very high crime rate. Some essential crime enforcement would help. I'd be happy to drive the cops around and show them where all the drug holes are. We could start there.

Every day I risk my life taking sketchy people down dangerous streets and through bad neighborhoods because the police won't do anything about it. We've had drivers robbed, shot, and killed; and the cops still won't step up enforcement in well-known crime areas. They want to shake my ass down instead.

JANUARY 18

I had a ride out to Madeira Beach and decided I'd go to a favorite place of mine. What made the trip special was that I hadn't visited there in about a year — Haslam's Bookstore, one of the few independents left.

When I came through the front door, I thought they'd stop me because I had a backpack, in which I keep my camera and gear. I carry the camera with me because I've been caught empty-handed too many times. Too many shots have slipped by.

I put down my bag to get a drink of water at the fountain, and when I turned around, a little kitty was inspecting it, sniffing, looking, pawing. *What is this?* he must've thought as he continued to nose around it.

"Well, hey little guy, let me show you," I said as I opened my bag.

As I said that, he jumped up onto one of the computer monitors. "Just stay perched there, and you'll make a great portrait." Photography is easy with such an agreeable subject.

I told him I had some catnip, so he was all mine.

I could see he had a great job. Everyone who came in the store wanted to pet him. Wow! To be loved all day long.

The lady who owns the store told me his name was "Teacup." His mother was a stray who showed up one day pregnant. They found homes for his littermates.

If this is some secret marketing strategy, like the big chain bookstores with their soothing music and coffee bars and overstuffed chairs, all designed to keep you in the store — it works!

I found myself in the American History section and spotted an out-of-print title I had to have. I was soon at the cash register, laying out the money for the book and saying goodbye to Teacup.

JANUARY 19

Martin Luther King Day. I was sitting on STAND 23 late this morning when a guy pulled up in a Toyota. He looked familiar, but I wasn't sure. He pulled up next to me, and I could see it was Johnny McPherson.

I haven't seen Johnny in about eight years. He used to drive for us but ran into some trouble after he hooked up with a crazy woman. He said he'd been living in New York and was doing okay. He was short on details, so I don't know what's going on with him. The reason he's in Florida is that his parents passed, and he's here to sell their home in Lake County.

I owe a lot to Johnny. He was my first friend when I moved back to Tampa in 1995, and he helped me get my first apartment. He was my neighbor for many years.

I got a call and had to leave, but not before giving him my number and telling him to call. Somehow, I don't think he will — just a feeling.

I told Larry, a real old-timer, about meeting Johnny, and he said: "Wow, I bet that was a surprise. I like Johnny. He just got together with the wrong woman. Where have I heard that before? Doesn't he have a brother in Brandon? Anyway, if by chance you see him again, give him my best."

JANUARY 20

A photograph in the *St. Petersburg Times* got to me. Two homeless people living in a tent city (forcibly removed by local authorities) are eating donated pizza by flashlight. The kindness of a stranger who dropped off several boxes of pizza affected me emotionally. I know there are many other benevolent souls out there.

As a photographer, I think this image tells a complicated story. It also shows why the city of Saint Petersburg should not have been so cold-hearted in closing down the encampment.

The reasons are obvious:

1) SECURITY: It's tough on the streets, and safety in numbers was a big help to many of the homeless people who were women, like Ann Rozelle, whose boyfriend was the last man to hit her. That was on Christmas Eve after beer turned to whiskey turned to vodka, and she says he took off his belt and whipped her in the face with the buckle. She ended up in the tent city. It was a safe place to stay till she could get her life back together. Her story was like so many women who fall in love with abusive men. Many of these women are frightened and unable to move on. Their desperation becomes a vicious cycle.

David Heath and Jeffery Schultz, who were residents of the tent city, were murdered by three teenagers out looking for vulnerable victims, but their victims had no money. What they had instead was a lifetime struggle with mental illness and substance abuse.

2) DIRECTION TO SOCIAL SERVICES

Many street people have no clue where to go or how to obtain help. If they're all together, social workers can begin to assess each case, identify their needs and getting them the necessary help.

3) FOOD: Like the stranger who dropped off the pizza, kind people can donate food. Where is all the money coming from? People have to donate if the government won't help.

I started a charity. I'm trying to raise money for the Metropolitan Ministries to provide food and toys for children next Christmas. So far, I have two donors for a total of $35. My goal is to raise $1,000 to help provide some real help for a few souls. The way the cab business is going, I might need the help myself.

JANUARY 21

I picked up a sad sack of a guy who was trying to get his stuff back from one of the run-down motels on East Hillsborough Avenue. This place is a dump. The cops took him away a few nights ago after he went on a crazy drunk. He gets a check the first of the month and blows it fast, so he's out of money.

He'll spend the rest of the month out on the streets. He's been doing this for years. People say they care, but do they? From what I see, there are many guys like him in Tampa.

The problem is that people like him make poor decisions that keep them down. The guy said he'd take real help if he could get it and paid me the last little bit of money he had. I felt guilty taking it, but I'm almost as bad off as he is. After getting his stuff back, he walked off with no clear idea as to what to do or where to stay.

JANUARY 22

I ran into old friends Patrick and Tammy this morning at Allied Cab. They've both been driving for decades. Tammy and I have gone camping many times, including her famous birthday party campout. I mention this because it's rare for cab drivers to participate in recreational activities. The ones I know don't want to get out of their cabs. Such is the subculture of taxi drivers.

Tammy is a late-night driver for Allied. She's been working for over twenty years and works only the night shift. Many people are surprised when she shows up or picks them up at one of our many strip and girlie clubs. They don't expect a woman. Nevertheless, she's tough and knows how to take care of herself and survive. She's no fool, and if a ride looks shaky, it's cash up-front. I like Tammy because she's strong, self-assured, and speaks her mind. She's out there every night and provides excellent service.

JANUARY 23

We see it all. We see the lonely, the desperate, the drugged-out, the stoned, the confused, drunk broads in crisis, the bullshit, the left behind, and the rejects.

Their lives are a metaphor for every back road, blind ally, dead end, and detour we take. We take them somewhere, but they're going nowhere. They're only creating the illusion of movement and accomplishment.

They tell the cabbie everything, things they won't tell their families, if they had families.

At first, I thought driving a cab would be cool. I only wanted to put the street beneath my feet, but I found out these are lonely roads. There are lights and signs out here, but none that lead you home.

There was a recent song, a jazzy, haunting ballad called "Cab Driver" by Daryl Hall. I've always thought the lyrics spoke to the concerns of many of my passengers: how they need the cab driver to take them home because they've been away too long. They've spent too much time alone, and only the cabbie can get them back to their baby.

What fares don't realize is by the time they get in my cab, it's too late. Like an episode of the *Twilight Zone*, I'll be driving them to another dimension in time and place.

JANUARY 24

At Tampa International Airport this morning, I was the first one sitting on the deck, which is a big parking lot where cabs line up, when Mack, the starter, radioed for me to pick up my fare.

There's a lot of anticipation when you're rolling down to pick up your ride. I have no idea where the passenger is going or if the time spent waiting will justify a short ride, something all drivers hate.

I had a passenger today who had to get to Sarasota, and

he had cash in hand. He worked for an auto dealership up in Ohio and needed to pick up a truck and drive it back to the Buckeye State. The estimate Mack gave him was $180. He didn't bat an eye (it's only short-fares that complain). All I had to do was figure out the fastest way to get there.

That's when it hit me: I'd have to cross the Skyway Bridge! I hate that bridge and have a real phobia about passing over it. I almost close my eyes when on the bridge.

In 1990, my twin brother, Tom, saw a guy park his car at the top of the bridge and jump. He told me the story the next day, saying, "I think I saw a guy commit suicide last night." Tom was driving over the bridge after getting off work at midnight in Saint Petersburg and was on his way to Sarasota, where we shared an apartment.

My fare and I were headed down the interstate, having a friendly conversation, but I was cognizant that we were getting closer. I was beginning to freak out. I didn't want to alarm my fare, so I tried to act brave with the bridge looming in the distance.

There isn't much to see on the bridge but the bridge. The water is way down there, and I tried not to look. I just kept talking and eventually we were on the downside.

I got the guy to his destination, and it ran $185. He gave me $200.

I was on my way back to Tampa and back over the bridge.

JANUARY 25

My former high school English teacher, Tom Stroup, left a comment on my Facebook page today. He said sometimes life is about the journey, not the destination. It gave me comfort to read that.

He's a very wise man and has been a father figure to me since I sat in his English class at Warwick High School in Newport News, Virginia, in 1974.

In the spirit of journeys, I went on a long hike on the Florida Trail. It was a beautiful day, temperatures in the 50s with clear blue skies — such stuff as dreams are made of. Florida stays hot most of the year and areas like this are typically overgrown, bug filled, and snake infested. As I've gotten older, I've developed an appreciation for the solace a place like this offers.

Smelling the roses is important to me now — not just for stress relief, as I fight high blood pressure, but for the enjoyment of the moment, the journey. I saw beautiful lakes, birds, a deer, and heard coyotes yapping in the distance. You don't have to be rich to enjoy a moment like this, and I was the only one out there. Nice.

JANUARY 26

I work the airport when I'm looking for a big score. When I work the streets, I can get bogged down in all the peripheral stuff that goes with it: no shows, little old ladies, no shows, grocery stores, no shows, and GNOMES (Got No Money).

At the airport that all changes. People are either going somewhere or not. Today the fares had places to go. The cash register kept ringing all day, and my hands were dirty from counting all that filthy money.

Between rides, I ran into Sam. Sam is from Iran. I've known him for ten years. Talk about a Renaissance man, this guy has been a professor and airline pilot and can speak seven languages.

On 9/11, I was wondering where he was. I knew he'd flown for Iran Air, and combined with the fact that Muhammad Atta received a hack license from the Tampa Public Transportation Commission, I was worried.

When I did catch up with him, he was laughing because he knew I'd think he was involved. Sam began to talk, or I should say lecture. His vast knowledge makes it easy for him to stray into heavy subjects — such as the Third Punic War's effect on 1st-century economies.

Well, the line at the airport was moving fast, and we were soon on our way. This time of year is pure gravy, and I couldn't help but think how busy Gasparilla will be in a couple of weeks with pirates throwing trinkets to drunk girls showing their tits for ten-cent beads, with about 500,000 revelers convening on Bayshore.

JANUARY 27

I don't have a category for weird, but if I did, this would be it.

Yesterday some people yellow-taped off the parking lot of the K-Mart at the intersection of Columbus and Dale Mabry. They said they were holding a "Car Show." Not much was going on until this tow truck showed up and delivered a little red car. After they unloaded it, people began hitting it with baseball bats, sledgehammers, and cinder blocks. What did that little red car ever do to them? They busted out the windshield and all four windows and put some serious dents in it.

Larry and I sat there watching because we were parked at STAND 23 and had a clear view of the spectacle. The people participating said they'd clean up the mess, but this morning the little red car was still there all smashed up. One might swear someone had used a monster truck to roll over it. How else could it've sustained that kind of damage?

JANUARY 28

Some gas stations in Clearwater are lowering prices at least 20¢ a gallon. I wish they were doing that in Tampa.

It amazes me how many people think the company pays for our gas. They act shocked when I tell them drivers buy their own. The price of gas is a big reason I can't make money anymore in the taxi business.

JANUARY 29

Today was pretty good. After running a drug addict to Saint Petersburg who amazingly had money, I went to the airport. Thursday mornings are always pretty good there. Other times of the week I can wait up to three hours to get a ride. Then the fare goes short. I moved quickly through and got three passengers going downtown, so for my two hours, I got about $80. Not bad. They even tipped well.

Later, I took a guy to work, and the meter ran $8.75. He gave me $9.00 and said, "Keep it." What he didn't know was he left his cell phone on the back seat. A few minutes later, I heard it ringing and picked it up. He wanted me to bring it back.

"Fine," I said. "Five bucks."

He called me a "white cracker motherfucker" and said he was going to report me.

He called the back office and talked to Marjorie, our office manager. She rang me on my cell, and I explained to her that he didn't want to pay the fee to get it back and that he didn't tip, which in my book makes him a worthless asshole. She agreed and said I could bring the phone to the office at my convenience. I will, but not until Monday.

JANUARY 30

There are wild chickens running around Ybor City. I guess they must've escaped years ago and now run free. There are so many of them, I see them everywhere. People like the chickens and put up CHICKEN CROSSING signs and chicken decorations in their gardens.

JANUARY 31

People will ask, "Can we go to McDonald's?" That's twenty minutes I'll never get back. There's nothing fast about fast food, and the fares are mostly drunk and annoying. Instead of waiting in the drive-thru, I could be picking up passengers and making real money. Stupidly I picked up these stoners and found myself saying into a drive-thru microphone, "Give me a number three with a Coke and a side order of extra large fries." Then, they spilled most of the shit on the back seat. Special sauce from Big Macs is tough to clean up.

All cabbies eventually learn the language of fares. For example, *I won't throw up* means I have only seconds to stop the cab and open the passenger door before they toss their cookies on the back seat. Some cities now have an extra charge posted on the window for cleaning up vomit.

Change for a hundred? means they're going to rob my ass and want to know if I have cash.

FEBRUARY

FEBRUARY 1

The Super Bowl was played in Tampa today, and like most Americans, I watched it on television through the fog of countless beers. The Steelers became the first franchise to win six Super Bowls, defeating the Arizona Cardinals 27–23. Ben Roethlisberger threw a TD pass to Santonio Holmes with 35 seconds remaining for the win. Sometime during the game, I heard a man yelling in the parking lot of the motel where I live, "Wha' chew want, bitch?"

FEBRUARY 2

After picking up a fare this morning, I heard chatter

on the radio about a bad accident on I-275. We went right by the spot, and I saw an overturned car. What I didn't realize was that it was an Allied Cab. There were about ten cars involved and the taxi got the worst of it. On the way back, I snapped a cell-phone image of a tow truck pulling the cab onto a flatbed. Dispatch never did update us on his condition.

FEBRUARY 3

On the back lot of Allied Cab, you can see the overflow of the Tampa Shuttle vans. These shuttle vans are a direct threat to our business. Free-market capitalism is great, but Allied Cab owns Tampa Shuttle. What do they care?

With so many drivers now, I must work harder and longer to make the same amount of money. Nowadays even these efforts don't help. A friend of mine asked me why I don't get another job. I told him I feel like the bank robber Neil McCauley played by Robert De Niro in the movie *Heat*. Al Pacino, who plays an LAPD detective, says to him, "Then maybe you and me, we should both go do somethin' else." De Niro replies, "I don't know how to do anything else." After fourteen years, taxi driving has become a part of me. It's my daily routine. It gives order and stability to my life. Like any addict, it would be hard to walk away.

In Tampa today, I saw numerous independent cabs, such as AFFORDABLE TAXI, ADDIS TAXI, AMERICAB, ABC TAXI, A-1 CAB, OLDSMAR TAXI, NORTHWEST ZONE TAXI.

Does Tampa need all these taxi companies? Most drivers are paupers. There isn't enough business out there to support such a swarm of cabs. I guess drivers are willing to work sixteen hours a day, seven days a week. Today, in the business office, I saw a group of men filling out forms to become new drivers. One guy said he used to drive in Boston, where you must own a medallion, which costs up to $750,000! That's insane! You can't earn that driving a cab. Allison once told me that in London, cab drivers train for two years to get a license, memorizing the city's labyrinthine streets, businesses, and landmarks. They must then pass the most difficult test in the world called "The Knowledge." In Tampa if you have a pulse, you can drive a cab.

FEBRUARY 4

They say you don't retire from the cab business, you just quit. Well, one of my best friends, Larry, turned in his keys today. He did it the right way by waiting until he was sixty-five with sufficient money invested. He should be all right financially.

One thing that makes this job interesting is the characters that sit behind the wheel. Larry was one of them.

He started in California, eventually living in almost every state, once working on an offshore oil rig in the Gulf of Mexico. He's been up and down, and it's good to see Larry retiring on top. I'll miss his daily friendship on the stands, but I'm happy for him.

FEBRUARY 5

I read a newspaper article about the great python hunt in south Florida, which has confirmed scientists' fears that pythons are spreading north in search of food. They're killing off small mammals, and they're tough to catch.

A recent month-long bounty with 1,500 hunters yielded only fifty catches. The park service estimates their population is over 100,000. It may take mother nature to get rid of them with frigid weather, but the weather has been sweltering at the only time of year when we should count on cold. Not much break there.

The failure of this hunt isn't good news. Who'd want to go camping when one of these things could get into your tent? Nothing good has happened by the introduction of this invasive species to Florida. The reptile lovers who let them go should've killed the snakes instead.

FEBRUARY 6

I don't care what any driver says. We're not having a tourist season. Cruise ship passengers on the weekend don't make a season. It's Friday morning, and no airport flights are going out, just like last week.

I'm not making money and am on the brink of eviction. I owe the company money, and I'm now wearing dirty clothes because I don't have the five bucks for laundry. I have nothing, and I work seven days a week, ten hours a day. Something is wrong.

After giving my landlord all the money I made last weekend, I had $3 for gas. I also needed to pay $182 to the cab company for the lease. I'll put in about twelve hours today and go home with three dollars again. This is what I do every day, and I'm getting nowhere. I'm like a hamster on a running wheel.

FEBRUARY 7

Gasparilla Festival was today, and I got a flat tire on the Courtney Campbell Causeway halfway between Tampa and Clearwater, so I was late to the event.

Not everybody who attended Tampa's Pirate Festival had the best of times. I saw many young women passed out. These ladies were doing it to themselves. I hope they recover and learn to party more civilly. I have tons of photos of litter and trash, beer cans, and half-naked people everywhere. That's the face of Tampa the mayor's office doesn't want you to see.

Traditionally Gasparilla marks the beginning of the tourist season in Tampa and used to be a productive day for Tampa taxi drivers. The problem is the police have been cracking down on open containers. They're also limiting the areas where people can drink. It's an adult party, but the local politicians ruined it. In the past, half a million people would show up. Today's attendance was down to 100,000. There was a time when it had the potential to be an event on the level of Mardi Gras, but that time is in the rearview mirror. The festival has been going on for over a hundred years, and it's now just a pissant local sideshow.

I wish I could be cheery about outdoor festivals, but I don't have a gig that can support me and it's weighing me down. I'm living in poverty. I can't overstate this fact.

Nevertheless, there's still beauty in this world. This morning I took a snapshot of the sunrise. I can only hope the sun shines from here on out.

FEBRUARY 8

The trip I got to Lakeland ran an easy $90, and the lady never batted an eye. One thing cab drivers hate is when a customer starts busting our chops because the meter is too high. We have nothing to do with that, and if passengers knew the outrageous lease payments we have to make to the taxi companies, they'd understand.

FEBRUARY 9

Speculation is booming in Tampa Bay real estate again. Corporations are buying homes, but nobody's living in them. These money grubbers are squeezing out families looking for a place to live. That's wrong. I thought we learned our lesson.

Home buyers now outnumber homes for sale, and companies with large sums of cash are squeezing out ordinary people.

Who are these cash buyers? A local news channel took a close look at bay area sales records and found something strange. Several investment groups, many based in Delaware, are buying up Tampa Bay homes. These are the greedy rich bastards whose avarice knows no bounds.

FEBRUARY 10

Why was it so hard to find a cup of coffee this morning? There was a water ban the past couple of days due to high levels of bacteria. The ban was lifted this morning, but none of the convenience store clerks were aware of it. I argued with them, but it did no good. They kept saying they had to wait for the manager.

So I went to an independent store owned by a colorful guy named Habeeb, who worked as a translator in his native Tunisia. He prides himself on the strength of his coffee, and this morning it was piping hot and delicious. On the TV above the counter, BAY NEWS 9 was saying the ban was lifted.

FEBRUARY 11

It'll finally get cold in Tampa. It'll now feel like winter for a few days, and maybe the tourist season will erupt. I still have a job and a place to live. It's one day at a time. I'll get through this and be better because if it.

Which is more than I can say for Wayne Tompkins, who was executed today by the state of Florida. Twenty-five years ago, he strangled his girlfriend's 15-year-old daughter, Lisa DeCarr, and buried her beneath the porch of their Seminole Heights home.

Prosecutors made the case that the girl resisted Tomkins' attempt to rape her, so he killed her, then told the girl's mother she ran away and was never coming back. Her remains were found a year later. It took him nine minutes to die from lethal injection at the Florida State Prison at Starke. The Tampa girl's family attended the execution.

FEBRUARY 12

I went to post up this morning at 5:09 A.M. and the system had blocked me. The message said: "See Ryan and Syd." That's a scary message to get. Ryan is the general manager of the company, and all I can do now is wait for daylight and management to show up.

I was thinking the problem was an oversight or error. I didn't want to jump to hasty conclusions when I didn't know anything.

I owe the company money because of poor economic conditions. I've been paying off my debt, including $200 last week. I hope the company isn't going to fire me after fourteen years of service.

When I finally spoke with Ryan and Syd, they told me they were suspending me. Being told to leave your job isn't easy to stomach. Their reason was that the new insurance company doesn't have my correct driver's license number, and they can't pull my DMV report. Without that, they can't insure me. It sounds like somebody fucked up, and it wasn't me. Now I'm home with no cab, no job, and no clear idea when I'll be back to work. As much as Gulf Beach Transportation tried to spin it, *they fucked up!*

You can't pass the buck when you're dealing with people's lives. I have a perfect fourteen-year driving record with this company, and they suddenly have no copy of my driver's license?

FEBRUARY 13

I got cleared by insurance, and I'm back driving. Plus, the company gave me a couple of free days to make up for it. As Shakespeare said, "All's well that ends well." Good timing because this is the season Tampa cabbies look forward to although it's been way off what we hoped for with few winter visitors. It can't be because of the weather.

The weather couldn't be better for our business. There are several feet of snow up north. Parts of the Northeast have huge accumulations of snow. The weather in Florida is balmy and humid. You can go swimming at the beach. The temperature right now is 80°. The sky is blue, and golf courses await. Still, nobody is coming down. People are still afraid to spend money — even rich people

FEBRUARY 14

I love mornings. The sun is rising, and there's a sense of optimism in the air. Saturdays can be slow, and this morning was no exception — not a single call until 6:32 A.M.

About the only thing I hate about Tampa is it's too seasonal. Your bills don't change, only your income — a lament heard throughout the Tampa Bay service industry. Even the strippers complain.

We used to get tons of rides from strippers who'd call a taxi to avoid stalkers following them from work. Many request a lady driver because some male drivers hit on them.

I should give my number out to more people, maybe have some business cards printed. I'm going to starve waiting on this dispatch system to give me a break. When I started driving a cab in 1995, we'd do 3,000 calls a day. Those days are long gone.

FEBRUARY 15

I got this newfangled cell phone last spring. I knew it took great photos, but I could never figure out how to download them to my computer.

I never bothered to ask another driver for help. Most cabbies know as much about computers as a kangaroo. Well, today I was at a favorite restaurant of mine on Kennedy Boulevard. The family that runs it is Cuban-Black, and they're cool and serve good food.

This morning, Los (who won the *Weekly Planet* award as best drive-thru attendant in Tampa) was sending an e-mail from the same type of phone I have. I asked him how he did that. I explained the problem I had with photos, and he showed me how to send an e-mail so I could download an image.

FEBRUARY 16

Presidents' Day. Why is it so cold in Tampa? Passengers at the airport ask me that question all the time. At least they admit it's subzero or thereabouts where they came from. Florida is the warmest spot in the US although temperatures this time of year are usually in the 30s in the northern part of the state.

I knew when it got cold up north, they'd be flocking down here, and they are. It did work against us, however. In the last two days, many flights were canceled because of excessive snow. Watertown, NY, was under twelve feet! That mucked things up for everyone. At least I wasn't on the planes sitting on the tarmac and looking like a scene from the A&E show *Airline*.

Even still, the rabbits are coming. A rabbit is a customer at the airport who's going nowhere. He barely qualifies for the $10 minimum for airport service in Tampa. He usually has on a business suit, no luggage, cell phone in his ear, and is walking very fast. He's beaten everyone off the plane to the taxi line. For whatever reason, he goes short. You can count on it. He tries to make you feel better about the situation by saying, "I understand it's only minutes away." Or the one I like: "Don't worry. It's not very far." Great. That'll put food on my table. For whatever reason, the cell phone never leaves the ear the entire time. It must be nice to be important.

I did pick up this family down from Pittsburgh who came to see their long-lost son. I don't know if he knew they were coming because everyone was hugging and crying and blowing snot everywhere. It was like one of those TV shows where they reunite people. I almost lost it watching it.

FEBRUARY 17

I picked up the guy who owns Geno's Pizza in Clearwater. When I dropped him and his wife off in Westchase just after sunrise, I couldn't get into the driveway because these huge birds were hanging around. They refused to move. He said they'd been hanging around for years, and the neighbors feed them. They were Peacocks. I'd never actually seen one before. I got out my cell phone to shoot a little video of the birds walking around.

FEBRUARY 18

I'm beginning to see construction jobs throughout Tampa. That's a sure sign of an emerging economy. In the last five years there's been nothing. I drive all over Tampa Bay and haven't seen so much as a porch remodeling job, but today I saw condominiums going up near downtown. Construction means jobs in the building trades. The only way to stimulate the economy is to put folks back to work, which creates a better dynamic than unemployment insurance. Let's hope we can build momentum.

FEBRUARY 19

The chess game against my old high school English teacher, Tom Stroup, is still in progress, and I'm playing him even. Tom is a chess master, rated in the top 2% of all players, so I'm happy for such a result so far. He's analyzed the remaining moves and sees this as a possible draw, but I can still screw this up.

FEBRUARY 20

I hate calls like this. I'm not out at 2 A.M. for my health. I need fares with money who're going somewhere. This call fit only one of those criteria.

A Southside bar known for a decent crowd was my destination as the bars in Tampa were closing. My fare was an older woman sitting at the bar. The hot-looking bartender said goodbye to her, and she seemed like a regular. She knew the routine and would have money. Wrong.

She asked me if I'd take her dead husband's watch as payment to go to the suburbs. What? I'm not Rick on *Pawn Stars*. This watch could be something she won in a 50-cent claw machine. What's next? A ring from a bubblegum machine. No thanks. She spent all her money at the bar and now wanted to cheat me out of payment.

I told her to get out, and she started crying. What was she going to do? Should I care? The circumstances of her being at that bar at that hour aren't my concern. The company will fire me if I continue to drop short of paying my lease.

I drove away, nevertheless feeling like a total asshole.

FEBRUARY 21

I had a run out to the Tradewinds from the airport. I made a point of stopping by the Don CeSar in St. Pete Beach. I always take a selfie in front of this grand pink hotel. In the photo, I look tired and need a shave.

I've been working brutal hours since they raised our leases again. This run only helped me cover expenses. The reason I haven't shaved is I keep forgetting to get razors and shaving cream.

There's no rest in this business. You get back up the next day, and you're at it again.

FEBRUARY 22

On Sundays I occasionally take people to the International Church. One thing I've noticed is the people I pick up are mostly minorities from Caribbean countries. I'm not trying to be funny, just an observation. If you drive by on a Sunday morning, you will see mostly poor people going into the services.

I had a pick-up there this morning after service. A family of Haitians wanted to go to Tampa Palms. They gave me a hard time on the way, and when we got to the apartment complex, the father wanted to be let out at the leasing office to get his mail, and the mother and the kids went to the unit building.

When they got out, she said she was going to get the money. She never returned. Since I'd lost sight of her, I didn't know which of the hundred units they disappeared into. At the leasing office, the man was gone.

All of this larceny *AFTER CHURCH!* I've never heard of such a thing. I think it may have to do with the way the church aggressively begs its congregation for donations. These folks simply don't have any money left. The church has tapped them out.

FEBRUARY 23

I saw a truck get sideswiped by an old dude and his daughter. I was at the intersection of Platt and Fremont, waiting to head south to STAND 21 when this car stopped on a dime in the middle of the road, turned sharply to cover two lanes, then slammed into a work truck, which then spun out of control and almost flipped.

I pulled off to the side and parked behind the truck, the first time I'd ever been angry after witnessing an accident. The daughter came over and said nobody was hurt and that I should mind my own business and move on. I said I was a witness and that it wasn't an accident.

Careless and irresponsible driving isn't an accident. I told her that her father doesn't know how to drive and almost killed someone. She started screaming at me in her New York accent.

When the cops showed up, I let them know what happened and was soon on my way.

I see this sort of thing every day: people crossing three lanes of traffic and stopping on a dime because they're going to miss their turn.

FEBRUARY 24

One of my best friends in the garage is Joe. He's not only a good mechanic, but he has a soft spot for birds. Like Shoe, he likes to feed the little sparrows that hang around Gulf Beach Transportation, mostly near the wall that gives us a little privacy.

One problem is the scavenger seagulls. These ubiquitous birds are always stealing the bread Joe throws out. He scares them away, but they're very adept at getting what they want. That's why I always wonder why tourists feed seagulls. These things never go hungry. They don't need to be fed. Feed the homeless instead. Come to think of it, sparrows never really go hungry either. They're just cuter.

FEBRUARY 25

I rolled into the Mons Venus strip club about four in the afternoon. I'd been dispatched there to pick up "Johnson." The club always puts the fare's name out as "Johnson."

This strip club is particularly famous for NO SHOWS and other things. It's on the main drag where cabs pass by all the time. It's easy for the fare to flag down the next taxi that comes along and hop in.

FEBRUARY 26

I see it every day in Tampa. They seem to be at every intersection, their pleas for help scrawled on the back of cardboard, as commonplace as traffic lights and stop signs.

Who are these people? What led them to the streets? Should I give them money? Something is amiss in America, some bad thing that's driving people to street corners and intersections; and in Florida, that means standing in the broiling afternoon sun in an attempt to survive.

Some people subscribe to the urban myth of the homeless guy flying a sign and making a couple hundred a day and then going home to his spread in the suburbs. I have my doubts. Flying a sign can't be a lucrative activity, considering the competition today. Some people believe that instead of money we should give them a bag with crackers and directions to a social center; but directions to a county office can't solve the homeless problem, which is chronic and systemic.

A few years ago, I considered these people bums. Nowadays, I'm not so sure. Driving my cab for twelve hours a day makes me familiar with these hapless souls. I don't think they're bums; they're the homeless and the unemployed. The ones I've talked to don't have jobs. At some point, people become unemployable.

A homeless guy named Billy hangs out at Hyde Park STAND 21. He talks to drivers and seems physically and mentally healthy. He's just *down on his luck*. He claims to have been homeless for several years and often panhandles for money. He survives, but that's about all he does. He's found places around downtown to get food. Some are better than others, but most places will feed the homeless and give them sandwiches to take. That helps them today, but what about tomorrow?

Billy goes on Sundays to a venerable old church near downtown called Hyde Park United Methodist. They feed the homeless on Sundays with a hot buffet of scrambled eggs, bacon, sausage, toast, hotcakes, juice, and fruit. I know because I've eaten there. The irony is that this act of kindness is in the shadow of swanky high-rise condominiums and Bayshore Mansions.

Many who eat at the church hang out and sleep on Bayshore or the entryways to buildings in East Hyde Park. They're now calling this area Homeless Hyde Park. It's a problem that's getting worse as time goes on. A homeless woman was killed by a hit-and-run driver in this area one night while crossing the street at the base of the Davis Islands Bridge, another ritzy area. The young woman who hit her has wealthy parents, and they hired a good lawyer to protect her from the legal system.

What these people need is *hope and change*. Maybe, one day, someone will come along and do something that'll give real hope to these people, like a job and a place to live.

My understanding is that we're in the worst economy since 1936. Over 250,000 more people lost their jobs in America last month, and there seems to be no end in sight. The unemployment rate is 9.8% and climbing. There are no jobs.

The homeless need work, money, health insurance, and drug counseling. Where are they going to get it?

FEBRUARY 27

There's a statue called Sticks of Fire located on the lawn of the historic Tampa Hotel, now part of the University of Tampa campus. It looks modern with seven bent pillars reaching toward the sky. The statue was the commissioned work of a Wisconsin artist who was artist-in-residence at the university. The *fire* term is the legendary Indian meaning of the word *Tampa,* "bringing light of knowledge and warmth of feeling to a people who don't just wish to exist, but to excel."

I went by the University today to take some snapshots. I had a fare there, and that's what I do. I shoot photos (at least I'm trying to get back into it). It was hot for a February day, and the sun was up high — not ideal conditions for a good shot, but I did what I could.

I did see something going on across the river at Glazer Children's Museum. Many people were milling about in the lawn by the river.

FEBRUARY 28

Islam believes in monotheism. That is, there's one god. All other deities are false gods or of the devil. Muslims proclaim this fact on the facade of their mosque.

"I'm the Lord thy God. Thou shall have no other God before me." Anything that comes between you and God is an idol and builds enmity with God.

You have to respect them for proclaiming their faith in such a manner. Cool architecture. A mosque (Masjid Omar Almokhtar) stands near North B Street and Willow Avenue, and it's common to see taxicabs parked out front.

MARCH

MARCH 1

I got a haircut. That isn't always easy. There are times of the year when I don't have the money. We pay a very high lease on these taxicabs, and most of the year there's no extra money. The same goes for laundry. I often wear the cleanest of my dirty shirts. Since the recession hit, lease, gas, and the number of cabs in Tampa have risen. The only thing that's fallen is the number of customers.

MARCH 2

My taxi was in the shop today, and I was driving a van instead. Around noon I was about to pull out of a motel parking lot. I looked to the left and right. No cars were coming — a rarity on Kennedy Blvd. I took my foot off the brake and began to press the gas pedal when suddenly I caught the image of a girl on skates streaking in a diagonal in front of me. I yanked the wheel to the left, almost flipping the van.

And she was gone.

MARCH 3

If you're an airport driver, you'll now have to wear what amounts to a uniform. You must wear the Allied Cab polo or button-down shirt. We can't wear shorts anymore, only long pants. It'll be hot, and I always liked the shorts option.

MARCH 4

A security guard held me against my will today. I was parked in holding at the airport when a man pulled up next to me and said he needed to return his car to National Car Rental. He wanted me to follow him to the lot, then take him out to the casino. Not bad. A $40 trip.

So I followed him. He dropped his car off, got into my cab, and we were on our way when I noticed the exit road was blocked at the airport service road. A security guard had turned his car sideways to prevent me from leaving. He told me cabbies weren't allowed in that area, and he wanted to see my driver's license. I showed him my hack license instead, something I'm required to do by anyone who asks. Only law enforcement sees my driver's license.

He insisted that if I didn't show my license, I'd have to go back inside and get an EXIT PASS, which was total bullshit. I said I was going to call the police and have him arrested for unlawful confinement. My passenger now got into the act and called him an *asshole dickface*. The wannabe cop finally let us out only after I began dialing 911.

As we left, he flipped us off.

MARCH 5

The storms were bad this morning. I picked this Haitian woman up around 5 A.M. She couldn't speak a word of English, could only point to where she wanted to go, which was North Willow, one of the most flood-prone spots in Tampa. It was raining like hell, and at one point the water was rushing like a tsunami. I thought the cab was about to be swept away.

The weather has changed since I moved to Florida in the late '70s, but I don't think it's the result of global warming. There are cosmic forces we're only beginning to understand.

MARCH 6

I was not trained in the ministry, or in drug and mental health counseling. I wish I'd been, for those skills are integral to my job. One would think my daily routine was passengers getting in my cab and telling me where they wanted to go; my taking them there; their paying me; and my being on my merry way. That's what happens most of the time, especially during the day when business people are on their cell phones and completely ignoring the taxi driver, but at night it's different. In many cases I'm called upon, directly or indirectly, to solve a crisis in a passenger's life.

One of the challenges facing social services is a real lack of funding. People in need of help are turned onto the streets. The cabbie becomes the social worker of last resort. I often encounter lost causes the system doesn't want to deal with or hasn't a clue how to help. That's when TAXI CHARGE VOUCHERS kick in.

Hospital emergency rooms have billing arrangements with cab companies. They give us a call to pick up patients (effectively dumping them onto us) and the cabbie goes and picks them up. Many times we take them to a mental health facility or alcohol rehab center. These state-run agencies can hold someone for only a few days, and then they're calling us to take those same patients to a flop house or cheap motel — like where I live. Considering most of those places are located in the worst parts of town, where drugs and vice are rampant, the odds of recovery seem long.

I got a call to pick up this woman at the St. Joseph's Hospital Emergency Room. The lady came out with a travel voucher in her hand. The address was to a local detox center. She looked a little nervous and shaky, so I asked her how she was doing. She said okay, and I proceeded to take her.

En route, she asked if we could stop at a convenience store. There was one up ahead, so I pulled in. She got out and went inside. I picked up the newspaper and started reading. A minute later I heard the back door open as she got back in. I started up the cab.

At this point, the manager came running out yelling and screaming in Punjabi-inflected English. "You fucking bitch! You pay for that beer, or I call the police."

I turned around and looked at her.

"Where's the beer?" I demanded.

She pulled it out from under her shirt and handed it to me. The manager was in my window, angry as hell. I handed him two bucks to cover the tallboy Budweiser and passed the beer back to her.

"Thank you," she said.

"Why did you steal it?"

"I don't have any money."

She started to cry. I told her I wasn't mad at her and that I knew what it was like to want a drink. Had she just asked for the money, I'd've given it to her.

On our way to the center, she told me everything that was wrong in her life. Her husband left; she hadn't seen her son in a year; she's a lush with no job, no place to live — you get the picture. Life is indeed tough for many people.

The thing about alcohol is that the individual develops a relationship with it. It's unlike other drugs. Booze becomes your best friend, at least, your most reliable friend. It's always there when you need it, unlike many of your human friends. When problems mount in life, the bottle is always there.

We pulled in front of the detox center. By now she'd regained her composer and finished the beer. She got out and walked bravely through the entrance. That did surprise me. I hope she gets the help she needs and pulls her life back together.

Many times I take people to these places, and they just walk off. They never bother to go in. They'll beg me not to take them there and want to be let off on some street corner where their clothes and belongings are hidden in a bush. I can't kidnap people, so I take them where they want to go and notify dispatch what happened.

MARCH 7

There was a bad accident on Dale Mabry today, so I pulled into the parking lot of Borders Books & Music and spent about an hour browsing. I bought the soundtrack to *Brokeback Mountain*. It's pure country, without a hint of homosexuality. Willie Nelson . . . Emmylou Harris . . . that sort of stuff.

MARCH 8

Tampa is a happening place with hipsters everywhere — in faded jeans, plaid shorts, T-shirts, beards, wool hats. They're all drinking craft beers, hanging out in coffee houses, smoking cigars, playing chess. They frequent the trendy Hyde Park, So-Ho, and Channelside areas.

Today, we were invaded. Hipsters from all over the country came to Tampa for two major events: the Gasparilla Music Festival and the Cigar City Brewery Festival. Both bring hipsters and money into the area. I don't know where their money comes from.

I mean the whole persona they exude is of slackers living off daddy's money and not giving a thought about the future. Well, whatever they figured out missed me by a mile. I work seven days a week and deal with stress I'd never encounter if I lived a normal life, but I do have a stash of illegal Cuban cigars.

MARCH 9

I had coffee with Regina this morning at Starbucks. In the past few months I've gotten close to her family, driving her husband, Donny, places *pro bono* because of their financial situation. She's been away for two weeks having a baby and dealing with some complications. The baby is cute. He'll be home soon, and his mother is doing well. Regina and her family have been a blessing and a real joy. She and Donny are young enough to be my kids, and I'm so glad to have her back in my life.

Cab drivers aren't allowed to contact charges on a personal level, but she sought me out and initiated the contact, believing I'd be able to help her and Donny. If you're a people person, this job will put you in touch with people going through life. Nothing will hit harder than life. You see that firsthand from the front seat. I know one day I'll lose contact with her, but for now, I enjoy her upbeat spirit.

MARCH 10

Nebraska and Florida Avenue, both north of downtown, are littered with old motels from the '50s. They're inhabited now by whores and crackheads.

As I stopped in the middle of the road to take a snapshot, a drag queen asked me for a date.

I should've known not to answer a call there. There are

only problems to be had, like the guy who maintained he didn't call for a cab although I had his name and cell phone number in my computer. Nevertheless, he insisted on flipping me off.

That's why I don't recommend this job to anyone. There are a lot of assholes in this world, and on this job I meet them all. A cabbie has to develop thick skin. That was tough for me to do.

MARCH 11

At the far west point of Cypress Boulevard is Cypress Point Park. This spot is a favorite for locals enjoying a lunch break and families relaxing on the weekend. It has beach access and a picnic area. I go their often when I don't have the time to go out to the Gulf Beaches.

This morning I had time to kill between rides, and I took a moment to photograph the beach after sunrise. With only a cell phone, I still managed to get some decent shots.

I was the first to arrive as the park ranger opened the gate. That's the way I like it. I don't have to deal with anyone on the beach, and I can set up my shots.

The sun rose on a beautiful day.

I soon headed farther down the beach to find some wading birds, mostly herons and gulls. In the photos, there's a splendid view of the Howard Franklin Bridge in the background.

MARCH 12

Morning rain in March means a cold front is moving through, which is good news. Two warm winters in a row have ruined the winter taxi business. I haven't taken a camping trip yet because I prefer the chilly, dry days we haven't been getting. I hope to go camping soon before the summer months are here.

MARCH 13

Today I drove a middle-aged couple to the Don CeSar out of Tampa International Airport. I needed that, for it put $80 in my pocket. I was behind on my lease and needed a break.

The prospect of staying in the crown jewel of Florida's Gulf Coast, spending a week watching the sunset over the Gulf of Mexico, excited them. There's much to say about decompressing like that. Sadly, that's missing from my nonstop life. I did let them know the Don was once a tuberculosis hospital. I hope that didn't mess up their vacation. They took it well.

Today was a good day. If I could string a few of these together, it would go a long way toward getting me out of the hole I'm in. Luck is a beautiful mistress, and I need more of her.

When I got back to the airport, the taxi line was moving fast — something we see during tourist season but not this time of year. I'll take the business. I need the money.

MARCH 14

I'm playing chess and working out to keep my mind and body sharp as I go through this difficult period. I just started playing blitz chess on chess.com, which is the best chess site on the Internet. It's where all the top players in the world play. The world champion, Magnus Carlsen, plays on this site almost every day. In a game last night, I checkmated a guy in five moves! I didn't think that was possible.

MARCH 15

I saw Syd in the break room today, and he seemed a little out of sorts. Not like him. He was dispatching today.

"People call in for a cab," he said. "And they feel there should be a cab outside the door. Right then and there. They phoned at the last second, but when you tell them you're sorry, it'll take 10-15 minutes, they give you an argument. I tell them there's no way we can make a car instantly appear in front of their door, and they get nasty and mad. And I can't get nasty and mad back at them."

MARCH 16

We've been swamped with business. Today was the first time in two years the airport was "King and Route." That's a term we use to mean it's so busy we can't handle all of it.

It's been a perfect storm of snow up north and warm weather in Florida, with Spring Break and all the arriving flights being full, but it'll be short lived. Were it this way all the time, I'd be a wealthy man.

What hurts us is we can't serve some of our regulars on time. The other morning I was on a two-cab call for a couple on their way to the airport to go on a ski trip to Colorado. Billy (one of our dispatchers) couldn't get another cab to respond, and the people said screw it, and they drove themselves. I wonder if they'll ever call again.

MARCH 17

I had a call this morning at 3:00 A.M. at City Side Lounge (gay bar) in South Tampa for Kim. I rolled up and told the valet I was there for Kim, and they loaded this finely quaffed guy in the cab. It turned out his name was Ken. I took him to his apartment.

On the way there, he said, "I wish I were straight."

"Why?" I asked.

"Then I won't be alone anymore."

He claimed it was easier for gays to get laid than straights, but what he wanted was to settle down. As he spoke, I thought that society seems tolerant of many things that were once taboo. For example, I remember a time if someone saw a shrink or went to AA or was gay, you didn't tell the neighbors. Now people can be open about these things.

I couldn't help this mixed-up guy. I only know that when love happens, he'll know it and it won't feel forced.

If you're looking for sex, that's a different story.

As a cab driver, I see the sex industry everywhere in Tampa. The people who work and patronize these places look lost. They look as if they'd give it all up for someone who loves them. Take the stripper at the Seven Seas whom I take home every Saturday night. There's real sadness in her eyes, and it's always there.

The Internet is where people are going nowadays. Just don't get taken. I have a friend who got burned on a Russian bride scam. He was so lonely and vulnerable that he sent thousands of dollars to a woman in Moscow. The money was for an airplane ticket. He never heard from her again.

MARCH 18

Tammy passed away of lung cancer. She drove a cab for twenty years to support her family. She was my friend, and we used to go camping together, which she loved doing.

What makes her passing even sadder was that she was looking forward to retirement and spending time with her grandchildren. She never made it. Chain-smoking is an affliction that many hacks deal with. Long hours, idle time, and boredom are the bane of a cabbie's existence. This unhealthy profession has claimed a lot of good folks in my years of driving.

When I first met Tammy, I asked her why she drove a cab. She said: "I like the flexibility. I'm a mother. When I first started doing this, I was a single parent. I wanted to get off public assistance and make a life for the children and me without relying on any state funding. I enjoy doing this. I enjoy meeting other people. I enjoy being able to work when I need to or work when I can. When I'm not doing this, I like to camp. I like to read. I like to hike. Eventually, I want to move to the Smoky Mountains."

I went to my laptop and tried to find images of Tammy, snapshots I've taken over the years. The only picture of her I found was a small low-resolution image. I have others on a thumb drive somewhere.

Of the many cab drivers I've known over the years, about half of them are gone. That's why I'm working on my health and exercising four days a week. I don't want to end up like most cabbies, who don't make it to sixty. The late fifties seem to be the end of the line. That won't be so if I have anything to say about it.

MARCH 19

Another small business closed its doors in Tampa. Crazy Ray was a nice man who served great sandwiches. I ate there at least three times a week. Their closing is another reason to support small businesses in this lousy economy.

I see people all day long lined up at McDonald's. Adults are paying what you'd pay at Ray's but getting crap kiddie food instead. It's neither cheap nor fast.

MARCH 20

I hate going to bars. It isn't true that hacks are happy to be designated drivers. It's easy cash, but no one enjoys the company of drunks. Bars closing late at night might be one thing. We can get people home safely, but a call to a tavern in the middle of the afternoon isn't good. Anyone shit-faced at 2 P.M. is an asshole.

Bars that call for a cab in the afternoon are usually low-end joints, and the drunk is often having personal issues they want to wash away. There's also not much money in this kind of call.

I got a call at a South Tampa watering hole for a guy named Edgar. I walked in and shouted, "Taxi!" I never know what's going to happen when I do this. Many times nobody responds. Then I yelled, "Taxi!" again, and after no response, I went over to the bartender.

She said, "Edgar, your taxi is here. "

I saw a guy at the end of the bar. He had a full bottle of Heineken he must've just ordered.

I walked up to him, and he offered to buy me one. I thanked him for the offer but told him I was working. He said he'd take care of me. That's the one thing cab drivers hate hearing because it's just drunken blather. I had a clue he might be different after I saw the keys to a Mercedes, which must've been the one I saw in the parking lot

I told him I'd take a Coke, and he prompted the bartender to give me one. I found out he was a retired Air Force officer with plenty of time on his hands to drink himself silly while he watched cable news and surfed the Internet, looking for conservative websites.

We finally left, and he told me where he lived. En route, he changed the destination — a bad sign. He now wanted to go to Tapper's Pub and drink some more and buy me a Reuben sandwich. One of the BIG FIVE RULES of cab driving is get a clear and precise destination. Without that, a driver begins to lose control. Security is always a concern.

I helped him into the bar because he was a little wobbly. I hoped they wouldn't serve him because most bars won't serve people if they're already drunk. They did, and I knew this wasn't going to be good. He ordered two sandwiches to go. I was now hoping they'd arrive before anything happened. Soon he started insulting everyone in the joint. It seemed like an hour when we finally got out of there. He tried to eat the sandwich on the way to his house but was making a real mess on the back seat. His wife was in the front yard as we pulled in. She looked a little disgusted but helped him out of the taxi.

Edgar gave me a $40 tip on top of everything, including what turned out to be a delicious Reuben sandwich.

MARCH 21

The Bay Walk area of downtown St Petersburg hasn't been a stranger lately. I've had many rides out of the airport going to Clearwater and the Gulf beaches. It's been so good I've wiped out a $1,000 shortage with the company, and at least for right now, I'm no longer fearful of losing my job.

MARCH 22

Ybor City in Tampa is turning gay, which is not a bad thing. For many years the nearsighted nightclub owners catered to young and underage crowds. Young adults have no money to spend and are only looking for trouble. They found it. Hardly a weekend goes by without a murder in Ybor.

The gays are well behaved and have money to spend. Everything from 7th Avenue to 17th West is becoming an exclusive gay zone.

MARCH 23

I had a ride today to a motel in Clearwater Beach. It used to be a quaint bed and breakfast but is now rundown and abandoned. Why? This was a charming place where vacationers spent enjoyable weekends, one of many mom-and-pop establishments that gave the area its charm. Now it's in the shadow of tower cranes building high-rise condominiums.

I once took a couple from Poland to a Clearwater motel which was Polish owned. The owners are a husband-and-wife team who do all the work and housekeeping. There's a swimming pool, and it's located only two blocks from a world-famous beach. How can you beat that? The owner told me a funny story that when they first moved from Poland, they'd put up a sign that said ROOMS FREE. What they meant was rooms were available. People came by thinking the rooms were free of charge.

MARCH 24

I came out this morning at 3:00 A.M., ready to have a good day. By 6:00 A.M. I had yet to get a single call. Not one. There was nothing even to bid on, nothing on the board. The conspiracy theory is that the morning dispatcher is playing favorites, using his cell phone to give his cab buddies the airport calls.

All I know is after many years in this business, I've never seen a morning I couldn't get a call before 6 A.M. How is that possible? Where are the calls? I quit around noon, with a total of four calls for $62. I'll be under if this continues. I'm getting worried. People say hang in there, tomorrow is another day. Unfortunately, each day seems to be getting worse.

MARCH 25

Strippers and cab drivers have a lot in common. We're independent contractors, which means we aren't paid a salary or an hourly wage. We pay the house to rent the space. In our case, it's the use of the vehicle. Strippers and cab drivers always seem to be struggling and just barely getting by. That's why I stopped listening to stories about how much money strippers make. Second thought, maybe I could take my clothes off and shake it on the weekends.

Many cab drivers will pull up next to you to talk in between calls and want to tell you how much money they've made or the big-ass trip they just took to Clearwater and the fare gave them a $50 tip. It's all bullshit. Most cab drivers live on the edge. It doesn't seem to matter how much money they book, they'll be broke the next day. Strippers are the same way.

I picked up a stripper who told me she made five hundred bucks the previous night. On the way to the club, she complained about her boyfriend, who doesn't work and just sits home all day and smokes pot. She's obviously pretty. I mean men pay her to get naked for them. She could at least find a man with a job.

When we got to the club, she told me she had to go inside to get the cab fare from the manager. What? She made $500 the night before and had to borrow money to get to work. She must be living like a cab driver.

MARCH 26

I dropped this guy off at his condo on Bayshore. I recognized him from the bus-stop bench ads all over town. It was the "Mortgage Guy," whose ads are all over town. He said the mortgage business is gone.

I pulled onto STAND 32 at Britton Plaza to chat with some drivers, and of course Emory, Bill, Ace, and Tony were parked there, griping about how bad business is.

With what's been going on the last three months, why would you park your ass on STAND 32? There are no major hotels or airports in that zone. Every time I work it, I get the little old ladies going to the doctor or the grocery store. Emory said things were bad, really bad.

Bill said he liked my shirt. It's the only shirt I have that people seem to like. So I had him take my photo.

Anyway, I left there and went to the airport and within minutes was on my way to Innisbrook Golf & Spa Resort with a $70 fare, and they gave me a large tip. The hell with STAND 32.

MARCH 27

Travis is a young guy, a graduate of the University of South Florida. He began driving a cab part time to put himself through school. Two years after graduating, he's still at it. He's good at what he does. He's been assaulted twice, robbed once, and estimates he's driven over 20,000 passengers. I had a quick conversation with him in the lot this morning and asked him if he was going to stay with the job. He said he planned on doing it for a while longer. "The job's biggest attraction is its flexibility."

Travis, like many, chooses to work on a casual or part-time basis. Taxi drivers receive no minimum wage, sick pay, health insurance, or vacation pay. They have no benefits at all. In many ways, they're the least protected workers in America, but drivers like Travis like it that way. They prefer the instant cash with no strings attached.

MARCH 28

A big mistake many taxi drivers make is not getting out of the cab. Exercise is essential, and walking is good cardio. The treadmill is annoying, but going out into nature allows me to hike for miles.

Today I began my search for Bigfoot and created a YouTube channel to document my adventures. If anything, I'll get some good exercise.

Tree-knocking is a technique that's been successful in contacting and communicating with Sasquatch or Bigfoot. It's believed the giant animal uses this as a way of controlling territory. I tried it today and had some success when something seemed to respond to my tree-knocking.

Today I drove out toward the Dead River. I parked the cab and wandered along a rutted dirt road. There were two drainage pipes that went under the road, which was once a creek bed. I headed back into swampier land, searching for an area that looked promising.

I set up a tripod and made a video, which I later uploaded to YouTube. It was the first one I ever posted, and in the video what's immediately obvious is how thick the saw palmetto is in Florida. Saw palmettos are essentially small palms, but they can grow thick and can push a hiker off a trail where they've overgrown.

There were leaves everywhere. February and March in Florida is when the leaves fall, and no matter where I stepped, the leaves *crunched*. It was quiet out there, pretty much a desolate area.

People aren't allowed to bring guns out here, but you are allowed to bring a baseball bat. I brought one for tree knocking and self-defense if necessary. I knocked on a few tress, and thought I heard faint knocking in reply. It's on the video.

I think I might've scared Sasquatch off. Who knows? Bigfoot will probably come up with a name for me now.

MARCH 29

Allied Cab tries to get all their inspections done before the end of March. Usually, when your cab is in service, they'll have the shop guys detail it, and then we take it down to the Tampa Transportation Authority for them to give it the okay. For the first time in fourteen years, I flunked!

The front bumper needed touch-up paint, the headliner was falling in the back, and the rear rubber seal was loose. Those things tear off when you load and unload luggage. I had mine just sitting there.

They should never have let our detail man go, Big Scott. He was a big Scottish man whose brogue was so thick I could hardly understand him. He used to come in every year during March and detail all our taxis. He did an excellent job, and I never heard of any cab failing. I think it had to do with money. What else? The shop guys don't care. Next time I'll do it myself.

MARCH 30

This morning I found a "suspicious package" tucked away in the arrival concourse at Tampa International Airport.

I took the stairs from the taxi staging area to the bottom floor where the arrival area is located. This is where the bathrooms are. Next to the service elevator was a brown box with two suitcases inside. They looked nondescript and too neatly packed for someone who decided to discard old luggage. In my years of working the airport, I've never seen anything like this.

When I came out of the men's room, the box was still there. The concourse was deserted. There was nobody on this level. Strange. Who'd leave such a thing behind? I didn't want to get paranoid, but why was it there? The overhead intercom kept repeating, "If you see anything suspicious, report it to authorities." That's what I was now going to do, but there were no security personnel to be seen. One would think that in light of 9/11, an airport would be crawling with security.

I almost started yelling, *Bomb! Get out of here!* I really did think this side of the airport was about to blow.

I ran into the terminal and found the courtesy desk and told the lady to call the police. She did, and it took fifteen minutes for them to show up. Finally, someone else showed up with a metal box on wheels and they hauled it away. It turned out to be lost luggage.

I was interviewed by a local television reporter, and it aired on the 11 o'clock news.

MARCH 31

There's a period between 11 P.M. and 2 A.M. when things are pretty slow. That's why when we get a non-tipping, going nowhere, drunk asshole, we cop an attitude fast.

I picked up this drunk woman at Ki Ki Ki III, a gay cruise bar. She went *exactly* $2.90. The meter only clicked twice! She then handed me a five dollar bill and said, "Give me back two dollars."

What should I have done? Thanked her for the 10¢ tip! She reasoned she often used Allied cabs and put a lot of money in Marjorie's pocket, but that's bullshit. Marjorie isn't getting anything from this woman. The cabbies pay the company a lease to drive. This woman was trying to justify being a cheapskate.

My next pickup knew how to tip and was more intelligent than the stingy lush. He was a producer for TBO.com, an excellent website owned by Media General. We had an outstanding conversation about website design — he was a cut above the average drunk. I took him to Seminole Heights. The tab ran $20, and he gave me $25. That's how you tip.

APRIL

APRIL 1

It's your gateway to Dante's hell for many people. When you're paying to go from Tampa to South St Pete to a dive motel, your life is already circling the drain. The cab driver is the Drano. I could tell when she got in the cab she was on drugs. I don't know what set of circumstances or poor decisions led her down this path, but I stopped caring a long time ago. I have to pay the vig or lose the gig. You see, I've got my own problems.

APRIL 2

I find it impossible to believe that I'm not getting

bids based on position. There must be something wrong with my cab, so I was going to shop it. I know how to drive a taxi; I've been driving one for fourteen years and know all the hot spots to sit and wait for a call. Youngbloods can't beat me at this game.

This afternoon I came across something on the lot that I didn't expect when I was looking for a new cab to check out. None were available. The economy is horrible, something this company has never figured out, yet they've been expanding — even in the midst of the worst economy since the Great Depression. Newspapers are already calling this the "Great Recession."

APRIL 3

The shop has been dicking around with CAB 363 since Monday. That was supposed to be my new cab, but they couldn't get it running. Our shop foreman, Syd, was good about it and put me out in a lower-mileage unit. The new car is sweet, and I hope to have a good weekend.

I like Syd. He seems perfectly at peace with his job, but it wasn't always that way. Once, during a slow moment, he told me that fifteen years ago, he had to take a leave of absence from the business.

"For two years I was out," he said. "But ever since then, I take things the way they go. People can scream at me all they want, and I just talk back nice to them."

APRIL 4

I received an e-mail yesterday from Robin "Roblimo" Miller, a writer of computer books. He gave me his phone number and invited me for coffee and a visit. I wasted no time in taking him up on his offer.

After dropping off a fare in downtown Saint Petersburg, I headed across the Skyway Bridge. When I arrived at his home, a friendly dog greeted me at the gate. Robin came out and invited me in, and we spent the afternoon conversing about a variety of topics. He proved to be an engaging raconteur. I also met his charming wife, Debbie, who's an accomplished artist. Their home is decorated with her work.

Before Robin became a professional writer, he was a limo driver. Today he regaled me with stories from his driving days.

As I was leaving, he gave me an autographed book he wrote about an operating system called Linux. The book included an instructional CD-ROM. I'll read it and see what it can do.

APRIL 5

Palm Sunday. I wasn't on my way to church but on my way to Myakka River State Park to do some Bigfoot hunting when some asshole rear-ended me on the interstate. Traffic had slowed down at the exit, and this guy must've been distracted, maybe on his cell phone.

I'm okay, but my neck hurts, and I feel a little confused. The amazing thing is that there was little damage to the back of my cab. His car was a mess, the hood popped up and bent, radiator fluid all over the highway.

I posted a YouTube video about it, which I shot with my cell phone. In the video, a state trooper is parked behind the guy in the emergency lane, writing him a ticket as long as my arm.

APRIL 6

The day after the wreck, I found my baseball cap on the back seat. That's how hard I got smacked. It turns out this low-life has some bullshit insurance company with a website that's down and a disconnected phone number. Just my luck that some hip-hopping jit slammed into me. What a fucked-up world we live in.

APRIL 7

I've had weird experiences with drunk females. I remember one night, I was driving two young women who started making out in the back of the car, and it went on and on, and soon they were feeling each other up. I looked back out of curiosity and said, "Can't you wait until you get home to do that?"

The woman directly behind me turned and slapped the back of the seat and said, "Just drive. It's none of your business what we do back here. We're paying you. We can do whatever we want."

Another time, I picked up this very drunk young woman who began to decry her life situation, then asked me, "Can you lend me a couple of bucks?"

"I don't have a couple of bucks to lend you. You're supposed to pay me."

"You do, but you just don't want to. Okay, can you give me a buck twenty-five so I can buy a beer?"

"You're supposed to be paying me, lady."

"Gimme a buck twenty-five."

I dropped her off at her apartment and took off.

APRIL 8

Remember when every city had an A&P supermarket. I remember as a little kid riding in the cart with my twin brother while our mother ground a pound of EIGHT O'CLOCK COFFEE, using the store's coffee grinder. This was long before Starbucks and home espresso machines. My mother brewed coffee in a percolator, which was about all there was back then. I can still remember how great that fresh-ground coffee smelled! Of course we kids didn't drink the stuff. That was for grownups.

I picked up this man the other day at the airport and took him to his beautiful home on the beach. It turned out he was a writer for *The New Yorker,* and he seemed interested that I had a blog. I told him the only short story from school I could recall was John Updike's "A&P." Updike's story spoke to me in a way no other story did.

"A&P" is about a young man named Sammy, who works at the local grocery store. His job is tedious and boring, but the people who shop there are even more so. One day these three girls in bathing suits walk in to buy some snacks. Sammy notices them, but not in the lustful way young men look at girls. These women represent something more profound. Updike details the people and items in the store, including a record bin containing albums with titles like *Tony Martin Sings* (this story is from 1961 after all). The manager of the store shames the girls for wearing bathing suits; and when they leave, Sammy quits his job in solidarity with them and runs outside to join them, but they're gone.

Updike is telling us that people follow predetermined rules, set paths, and similar habits. The individual has no role in this society, and any attempt to escape these established norms is futile. Sammy wants to be a nonconformist. It's the nonconformists who've changed this world.

Starbucks doesn't serve EIGHT O'CLOCK COFFEE, but the hipsters who frequent the place are no different from the squares in Updike's story. Their SUVs look the same, as do their J.Crew clothes, laptops, bottled water, pedigreed dogs, and every other damn thing about them.

Follow your path, I always say.

APRIL 9

I've always been interested in Bigfoot research. In fact I still have the original *Saga* magazine that got me hooked. I was 17 years old, and I used to get that magazine every month. Because there was no Internet, print media were the only means of keeping abreast of whatever you were interested in, and I was always interested in Bigfoot, Loch Ness Monster, UFOs, that sort of thing. *Saga* never disappointed.

One month they ran a cover story about a young 25-year-old Bigfoot researcher named Tom Biscardi. This was 1973, and Tom Biscardi was flying in an airplane in Alaska at night with his research partner, and they were using what was state-of-the-art thermal imaging. I thought it was cool the way they were flying right above treetop level, aiming the camera down, trying to locate Bigfoot. I think I knew then that one day I'd get out into the woods somewhere and start looking.

APRIL 10

I picked up what appeared to be a successful young couple. They were well dressed and looked healthy. The guy started questioning me about taxi drivers.

"Most of you cabbies are derelicts," he said.

"Why do you say that?" I asked him.

"You don't have a job, so you go drive a cab. Anybody can get a license to drive a fucking cab."

"Have you ever considered driving a cab for a living?"

"No," they said in concert.

"Why not?"

"We have an education," the lady said. "I'm not putting you down."

"That's fine," I said. "I'm actually a philosophy major."

"What can you do with that?" she asked.

"Drive a cab," I said.

"It's scary, isn't it?" the guy said. "I keep up with the news. Like when that old cabbie got his testicles cut off. That's some scary shit, man."

APRIL 11

Candy has been on the streets for at least twenty

years. Longtime cab drivers know her from Kennedy Blvd., where she works as a prostitute. She's mentally ill and unpredictable, yet also sweet and friendly.

I saw her today for the first time in a year. I was at a gas station, and she asked me for money. I didn't have any to spare and told her. She looked unhappy and walked off.

APRIL 12

Easter Sunday. This morning when I was down at Ballast Point for the Easter Sunrise (found myself alone), I sat on a picnic bench with my 7-Eleven coffee and began to think about life. I mean, why suddenly do I want to turn everything up a notch. Aren't most men in their fifties scaling back and beginning to think about retirement?

Why is it that when you reach a certain time of your life, a time when you're more equipped to deal with it, your mortality begins to set in? Do I have only a couple more decades left? I'm just getting warmed up and hitting my stride.

APRIL 13

There's an urban legend that taxi drivers rig their meters. This isn't true. The meters are calibrated out of Tallahassee by the Department of Agriculture and Consumer Services. The meters are sealed, and if anyone tampers with them, they'll go to jail.

What they used to do when they inspected the meters was set up a road test of a measured mile. The hack would roll in, the inspector would get in the cab, the hack would drive the course, and if the meter said the right amount, the vehicle passed. Simple as pie.

Now, the testers are going high tech, using computers, and what used to take about ten minutes, now has drivers waiting in line for hours. Progress, I suppose.

APRIL 14

My job is inherently difficult. Taxi drivers face strange and deranged people daily. Taxi companies must serve the general population. We have no choice. Short fares, drunk fares, people going to buy drugs — we pick up all of them. There are also business people, beautiful women, day-trippers, and long hauls. The difficulty comes in not knowing if you will make any money. For someone with the personality of a gambler, this job is beautiful. I'm getting older, and risk is not my favorite hobby anymore.

APRIL 15

My friend Tony died yesterday of a heart attack. Apparently he was taking out the garbage and never made it. He was a guy everyone knew and liked. He was an old crab apple, but he was in poor health, which must've affected his mood. He was one of the longtime drivers from way back.

Tony came to Florida as many do in search of a better life. Those were the days when they said you got paid in sunshine. He'd already been driving a cab for fifteen years when I started, having worked the airport for ten years, then becoming a night driver. The thing about Tony was that no matter what he did, he couldn't get ahead.

I enjoyed my conversations with him. He often expressed a desire to work in the hot rod industry. He was an expert in vintage cars but could never get his finances right to move to California. "That's where the action is," he said. Instead, he stayed in his cab till the day he died.

That's a fate that awaits many cab drivers who get into a sense of denial about just how bad things are. I promised myself I'd never do that, but circumstances have given me no choice.

I hope they don't find me dead in a motel room. That isn't the most dignified way to go, but it's happened to way too many drivers.

APRIL 16

At home I'm always on the computer. It used to be if people took photos, all they had to do was have the film developed, then go shoot more pictures. Not anymore.

Technology was supposed to make our lives easier and more efficient. I'm afraid that's not so. I put in 4–5 hours a day just editing my blog, checking e-mails, viewing specific photo sites (no taxi sites), and trying to learn what I can.

And that's on top of working ten hours a day, late nights, weekends, and holidays. Plus, I pay the bills, cook the meals, do the laundry, run errands, and try to get some sleep!

Now I know why my twin brother is doing so well: he has a wife, a real partner, someone to chip in and help. They're a team, Tom and Sandy. They have a nice life out in California, where Tom teaches high school English.

Oh well. I tried marriage once when I was younger; it didn't work out. We were way too young. The wedding took place in the living room of Sherry's mother's house in Winter Haven in 1979. Tom was my best man. I was twenty-two; she, nineteen. As I said, we were way too young. We were divorced within a year.

APRIL 17

When the former manager of Allied Cab suddenly left a few years ago, Ryan Percy and Syd Glaston took over. They have a completely different management style. They're very accessible, and Syd always keeps his door open so any driver can walk in and state what's on his mind without any fear of reprisal. That couldn't have happened under the old regime.

APRIL 18

I'm mostly confining my searches for Bigfoot, specifically the Florida Skunk Ape, to the watershed areas of the Green Swamp and the Myakka River.

This is logical, for a large primate needs an abundance of water to survive. With the current drought, this area is becoming tighter and favorable for Bigfoot hunters. The reasons for looking in the Green Swamp of Florida are clear. The Green Swamp ranks second only to the Florida Everglades in terms of hydro and environmental significance to the state. Overlying the Floridan Aquifer, the Green Swamp ecosystem is important for the preservation of clean potable groundwater.

The Swamp also includes the headwaters of various rivers, including the Hillsborough and Withlacoochee. In the upper reaches of the Green Swamp, the floodplain forests and marshes promote natural retention of flood waters and provide habitat for many wildlife species. Habitats within the swamp include a mosaic of cypress and hardwood forests, pine flatwoods, prairies, and sandhills.

APRIL 19

The night air can become intoxicating and alluring to taxi drivers. There was a several-year period when I worked mostly nights. At first, the money was good, but there were other benefits: the roads are empty at night, and the vibe is different.

During the day, people are going places to engage in the routine activities of their lives. They'll go to work, the doctor, the airport, laundromats, and grocery stores. At night, people change. People go places because they want to. Frequently, alcohol is involved. Morality isn't always their prime concern.

Early in the evening, I picked up this guy in Palmetto Beach, and he wanted to go to a dive motel in Tampa. On the way up the interstate, I could see the expanse of Ybor City and the eastern end of downtown spread out for miles against the setting sun. Much of it looked like a glinting promise of better days ahead. It was exciting to see the city like this.

I was beginning to smell the night air.

APRIL 20

The *St. Petersburg Times* ran an article about the state of taxicab companies and drivers in Hillsborough County.

They quoted me in the article because I blog about cab driving. The article hit hard on some authentic aspects of the current state of the business.

Jack Nicas went all over Tampa, talking with taxi drivers and cab company owners. He went to the holding area at the airport, the major hotels downtown, the clubs on the weekends, and he saw firsthand what goes on in our work.

"'There was no concession on their part,' said Tim Fasano, an Allied Cab driver who blogs about the industry. 'Times have never been better for them. They have more drivers than before the recession, and they're getting higher leases now.'"

One thing I'll never understand, and my experience in life still leaves me with no reference point to make a judgment, is why do so many grown men continue to work under these circumstances? I'm one of them, but I thought half these guys would quit when the recession took hold. I was wrong. They keep driving and driving and driving, unaware that kids at McDonald's make more money.

APRIL 21

I thought of Ted today. He was an Allied Cab driver for almost twenty years. He was originally from Wisconsin and hadn't seen his family in years. He was very educated and once was a teacher; but like many in this industry, he became marginalized by society and continued driving. He left taxi driving behind after he ran a red light and broadsided another car. The accident was captured by a local news crew videoing a story in a nearby parking lot. The video went viral. Ted went missing.

APRIL 22

Almost nobody gets in my cab and talks to me anymore. Within seconds, they're on their cell phone. I bitch about this because one of the perks of the job was the conversations drivers had with fares. That's mostly gone now.

Today, at Tampa Airport, I picked up this businesswoman who was on her way to a meeting. She mumbled a location to me, and within *one second* was on her phone. I didn't know where this place was, so I had to interrupt her. She seemed a little annoyed. The problem is that we've entered into a business relationship, and I think she should at least take fifteen seconds to get clear with me on what I can do to serve her.

On the way to her destination, she called several people to let them know that she'd e-mailed them in response to their e-mail and was texting about the text she got about an e-mail.

There's a time management book by Julie Morgenstern called *Never Check E-mail in the Morning*. It's about doing things that, at first, seem counterintuitive, such as working fewer hours a day and spending only ten minutes a day on your cell phone. The author's premise is simple: save it for the meeting. Cultivate real relationships.

APRIL 23

Many drivers still sit on the old STAND 21 in Hyde Park. The stand is centrally located for getting calls. There's shade, a basketball court, a baseball diamond, and some cool wildlife. The retention pond behind the chain link fence is the home of many migratory and wading birds. Ted used to say they eat frogs, which are plentiful in the lake.

This pond has formed an ecosystem, and I wouldn't be surprised if fish were thriving in it. Every time I stop by, I see different birds. They know there's food in there, and they're patient enough to wait.

There's a hobo encampment behind the pump house. These guys aren't hurting anyone, and they don't bother people for money. Their camp is along the railroad line, where it's open and provides them with some security. They've collected several mattresses and a sofa. At least they don't have rent to pay. In many ways, they're better off than I am.

APRIL 24

I picked up three young women and drove them to Club Sky, a hip-hop club in the heart of historical Ybor City's entertainment district.

One of the women dropped the F-bomb with such staccato regularity that by the time we reached the club, even I'd had enough.

"Lady, you've got a foul mouth! I really don't appreciate that kind of language."

She seemed taken aback by my reprimand, perhaps unused to being upbraided for her language.

She exploded. "Fuck you! I don't give a damn what your cracker-ass think. This is how black people talk, so your honky-ass need to get used to it."

"Ma'am, the fare is twenty-six dollars."

"Fuck you! We ain't payin'."

They climbed out, leaving the doors wide open, laughing at my inability to do anything about it. I got out and closed the doors, thinking the cab's springs were happy to be relieved of about seven hundred pounds.

APRIL 25

Things aren't going well. I worked today from 4 A.M. till 2 P.M. and drove only eighty-nine miles. You can multiply miles driving by 1.1 for a reasonable estimate of dollars booked. Barely over $100. The problem is I pay the company $92 a day, and I buy the gas. Sounds like a great deal, right?

I'm a veteran cab driver, and I'm at the end of my rope. I need to sleep and have a semblance of a life, but I'm stuck.

I have no spouse or anyone to help me. I often wear dirty clothes because I don't have any quarters for the laundromat. I do have a five-dollar bill in my pocket, and that's it.

I only have one pair of shoes, which I'm using Gorilla Super Glue to hold together. Shortly, I'll be wearing socks. The difference between living in the Depression and my life now is they didn't have Gorilla Super Glue in the 1930s.

APRIL 26

Sunrise is always an optimistic time. You can be hopeful for a good day because much is unknown at this point. That's what makes cab driving exciting. I don't know what will happen next. It's like baseball during spring training — hope springs eternal.

Yesterday I got a charter. I haven't had one in a good decade. I quoted the lady $40 an hour, three-hour minimum, and you can't leave the county. She was only going shopping. It took about an hour, and she still gave me the $120. You can't beat that.

APRIL 27

"Just fill it up and bring it in." That is what our office manager Amy told me when I was giving her a ride downtown to go to the tag office. She had a new car ready for me and said she could trade me out for it. I began to think about it and realized that to fill it up would run me about $50-$60.

Thats a lot of granola. When I started in the business in 1995, you could begin the day with a full tank, damn near run it dry, and then fill up for $17. Now I spend easily $250 a week in gas. That goes right off the top. It hurts my profit and now my lifestyle.

Why are people still driving those big SUVs. They're not necessary. I remember when Jimmy Carter was president and the cost of gas rose to over a dollar a gallon, people started driving Toyotas and Nissans. They were willing to make a sacrifice. I see no evidence that today's generation is willing to make any sacrifice.

APRIL 28

One of our dispatchers, Ibrahim, has been trying to break into comedy for the last couple of years. Ibrahim is from Pakistan and goofs on his own culture and what it's like to be a cab driver in Tampa. All the best to anyone trying to better himself.

Tonight I dropped by the comedy club where he was performing and caught the show. Ibrahim is a funny guy. I liked his routine a lot. Some of it went like this:

"I know what you're thinking, and you're wrong because I'm not that guy from the 24-hour CVS pharmacy, and I'm not going to drive you guys home later tonight. I'm not that guy. My job for eight hours is, 'Excuse me, you paid for pump number 2, and you're at pump number 4. . . .'"

You had to be there.

APRIL 29

I picked up Elvis today, that is, a guy who looked like Elvis. There was a reason for that: He's an Elvis impersonator. He performs at local clubs, and is trying to break into Las Vegas. Like me, he has his goals. I told him I wanted to be a park ranger one day. He also gave me an autographed picture of himself with a motivational quote on the back: "To Tim, Keep on cabbin' & be livin' your dreams becomin' that park ranger. Keith Elvis Castro." He's a bit of a preacher as well and he believes all things are possible with the Lord. Everyone has to have a bag. At least he has one. I do want to get his CD of Elvis hits.

APRIL 30

I've been playing more chess lately on chess.com.

I'm currently rated almost an expert with a 1975 Elo rating, which puts me in the top 99.4% of all chess players in the world. (The Elo rating system is named after its creator, Arpad Elo, a physics professor.) The ones left above me are IMs and Grand Masters, and that's going to be a tough nut to crack.

M A Y

MAY 1

Once in a great while, the storms of change will overshadow the plans of man. A cold wind blew over Tampa Bay this morning, a brief respite from the subtropical heat. The cool air felt good on my face and lifted my spirits. I needed a lift.

I had a ride out to Boca Ciega, which is a beautiful area. It was a scheduled trip of some significance, and I felt hopeful. This ride would put some serious money in my pocket. Today was going to be a good day.

Hernando de Soto, the Spanish explorer and conquistador, once landed in this area. It was all jungle then and inhospitable to his gallant crew. Today, it's airy homes, many built in a time of no air conditioning, but the natural winds of the bay during storm season will cool off homes near the shore.

Homes built by the bay are buffeted by summer squall lines that move in fast. The wind and rain can be brutal. The clouds eventually roll offshore, and a couple of hours later, they cast oranges and reds for a beautiful sunset. This pattern repeats almost daily.

The sky was clear, and the birds celebrated the new day by soaring high, just like my hopes. I needed a good day to make up for all the no-shows of late.

The trip was scheduled to go out of town. I arrived on time to see no lights on inside. It was a quaint, charming cottage across from the bay, a typical Key West home with a wide porch, wicker furniture, wind chimes, and other bric-à-brac — the things that bring comfort to the soul and a sense of the spiritual.

I knocked on the door and noticed the artwork hanging inside. People with this kind of money usually don't call for a cab; but some people, for whatever reason, don't drive. I stared at the artwork and wondered what decisions the owner made that resulted in the direction his life took. He went on a path much different from mine. I wondered if he had a clue as to how important it was for me to pick him up and take him where he was going. Thoreau said, "The mass of men lead lives of quiet desperation." Did the homeowner know how desperate I was?

He answered the door in his bathrobe — never a good sign. He said his doctor's appointment was rescheduled for the next day. He wanted me to cancel the order. Great. Just what I needed. A careless act of no significance to him. Devastating to me.

MAY 2

I was sick in the ER today. My head was swimming;

I was off balance; I have high blood pressure; I was in trouble. Sam gave me a ride to the ER. The good news was they could find nothing wrong. My meds have my blood pressure under control and my motor skills were good. Their best guess was an inner ear issue, and the ER doctor told me to see an ENT specialist.

While this was going on, the company had someone drive my cab back to the shop from the airport. They thought I was dead and were about to cancel my contract in order to lease the cab to someone else (the entire process took four hours).

They have a waiting list of potential drivers, and they're eager to lease out any spare cab. In fact, if you break down, there are no replacement cabs. None. All cabs must now produce income.

I have a $500 cash bond and they could've waited a few days to see what my status was. They could've gone by the hospital or called me.

The company has always been good to me over the years, so I'll give them the benefit of the doubt and say there must've been some confusion about my status.

I walked four miles from the hospital to the shop to get my taxi back. If I'd died, my body wouldn't have gone cold by the time they had another hack behind the wheel. At least I know where I stand after fourteen years of complaint-free service. I deserve better treatment than that. I've earned it. This was an outrageous thing for them to even contemplate.

I did get my taxi back, but now I'm upset and believe I face an uncertain future. I have no insurance or company benefits.

MAY 3

In the last weeks, two Tampa taxi drivers have been found dead in their cabs.

People at the airport thought a 48-year-old Bay Cab driver was sleeping in the holding area. Cars just kept going around him. They went around him for seven hours! Nobody bothered to peer inside his cab until about 9 P.M. when a cabbie looked through the driver's side window and saw him slumped over dead.

Last week a cab driver pulled into the Radiant store at the corner of Kennedy and Howard to get gas. He sat in his cab for thirty minutes. My friend and fellow taxi driver, Sampson, was inside prepaying for gas when the manager asked him to take a look at the driver. Sampson found him dead inside.

Cab driving isn't a healthy lifestyle. Drivers smoke and eat the wrong foods and gain weight on the job. Most drivers who work seventy hours a week don't have gym memberships. It takes a toll.

I recently joined a gym, and I'm trying to establish a routine of weight and aerobic training. I have to do something. I don't want to be the next guy found in his cab.

MAY 4

Someone shot and killed Nigerian cabbie Cyril Obinka while he drove his cab last night.

About 9:30 P.M. his cab veered out of a parking lot at the Palm View Apartment Complex and crashed into a building.

Arriving officers thought it was an accident but called homicide detectives when they spotted blood all over the interior of the cab.

Cyril moved to the United States about a decade ago. He worked hard and saved money, recently buying a house. He'd been robbed on the job three times but continued to drive a cab so his wife would be able to stay home with their first child.

He dreamed of the future he would have with his family, but it all came to an end with a single gunshot to the upper body.

Police are asking the public for any information.

MAY 5

I went over to Edgar's house today. (He was the man I picked up in a bar last March, the guy who bought me a Reuben sandwich.) Last week he called Allied Cab to have me drive him to a Tampa Bay Rays game, with a ticket for me to accompany him (he needed a designated driver). I've become his chauffeur and friend.

Today was Cinco de Mayo, and I had an idea he'd be quaffing many a beer, and of course, the fridge was filled with Heineken, his favorite. We sat around, shooting the breeze and drinking from the cold green bottles.

His wife, Debbie, joined us. She's also his girl Friday and does many things for him. He's fortunate to have her.

It was good to see the both of them.

I'm jealous of Edgar's computer set-up with high-speed Internet. My dial-up is extremely slow. Edgar has Road Runner, and tonight I was able to get some things done on his computer. I need to hang out more at his place.

MAY 6

About 4 A.M. I got a call on the east side of Tampa at an upscale gentlemen's club. Déjà Vu isn't on the strip, but it does a big business.

The fare got in and said he had to go to the Homestead Inn in Brandon, get his bags, and head to Tampa International Airport for an early flight. He seemed a little agitated.

I asked him what was up, and he said the club was threatening to have him arrested.

"For what?" I asked.

"Soliciting prostitution."

Apparently, homeboy thought his generous tipping entitled him to something more than a lap dance.

After he paid his way into the VIP ROOM and dropped $200 in tips, she agreed to leave with him and go back to the hotel. She went to the dressing room to change into her clothes. He went out to the car to wait for her. She never came out, having left by way of the back door.

He went back inside and asked the manager where she was, but she'd already spoken to the manager herself and told him he was soliciting her. The manager threatened to call the police, so he left.

He asked my opinion if he was breaking the law. I told him, "A little bit."

When I asked him what he did for a living, he said, "A lawyer."

Imagine that. Anyway, I got him to the airport on time. It was the least I could do.

MAY 7

I dropped a fare off in Lakeland today. It's a small city in Polk County. I lived there in the late '70s and early '80s, and at that time it was a sleepy little town. I'm glad to see it's coming of age. I could see new growth and a real effort at gentrification typical of cities that have it on the ball. It now looks like the place I wish it'd been twenty years ago.

MAY 8

When I was leaving The Sunshine Cafe this morning with my take-out order, a cute little boy tried to hand me some cash. His father had given him the money to pay for their breakfast, and the little guy thought he was supposed to give the money to me.

Outside, I talked with the father, and he said he ran a blog about having breakfast in Tampa Bay. It's called, not surprisingly, *Tampa Bay Breakfasts*.

Andy Seely writes reviews of area mom-and-pop breakfasts, but most importantly, he writes about bonding with his boys. I miss the glory days of the Tampa Bay blogging scene when *Sticks of Fire* was on fire, and there was no Facebook. Social media destroyed blogging.

He posted a photo of his son and me. He wrote that his son "promptly tried to pay this cab driver picking up a takeout order. Shows how good Tampa's cabbies are. The man said, 'Look, kid. For $20 I can take you to the airport, but no farther.'" He must've used his cell phone because the image is a little blurry. That's okay. He doesn't claim to be a photographer.

MAY 9

I had a pickup at the IHOP on south Dale Mabry around 3:45 A.M. A very drunk gay man came out of the restaurant and wanted to go to Clearwater.

Over the years, I've been the victim of "cab beats." I've analyzed the profile of the people who beat me, everything from race, gender, age, sexual orientation, public or private residence, and so forth. The common denominator is age. The younger they are, the more likely they are to run. Never had a gay or older man run on me. That was about to change tonight.

This guy was singing a song that I recognized from *La Cage aux Folles*. He couldn't believe some macho-looking cab driver would know that. He seemed harmless even though he offered me oral sex and said he'd make me spooge ten feet. I respectfully declined.

When we got to his condo, he whipped out a credit card. I was glad that was the only thing he whipped out. I ran it with my cell phone — declined.

I then told "Michael D. Parker" he owed me forty-six bucks!

He said, "Fuck off."

He left the cab and went into his condo.

I followed him and pounded on his door. He refused to

open it, and when the light came on in the window, I peered in. He was cooking eggs over easy. Apparently this guy had a reputation at IHOP, and they wouldn't serve him.

I called the police.

When the cops got there, he refused to answer the door. The cops said there was nothing they could do and left.

So it goes, Kurt Vonnegut famously said.

MAY 10

Mother's Day. My AC went out this morning. Bad for two reasons. It's starting to get hot, and there's smoke in the air from wildfires burning in northern Florida. There was no freon in the system, and they had to repair a leak. Usually, I'd mind, but today was slow because of Mother's Day. Our afternoon dispatcher, Pirate believes the three slowest days of the year are Easter, Mother's Day, and Christmas.

While I was waiting, Shoe, our weekend dispatcher, came out to smoke a cigarette and told me he'd just seen the SHORT LIST. That's a list of drivers who pay on a 24-hour basis. Today the list was short, the clearest indicator that business has dropped off.

I wish they'd stop hiring so many new drivers. The job doesn't pay shit, and I'll be damned if I understand why men will travel halfway around the world for a pauper's wage. Does it suck so bad where they came from that they find it necessary to take the bread out of the mouth of guys like me? It makes no sense.

MAY 11

I had a run last night to Wesley Chapel and back to Tampa. By the time I got back, the windshield was covered with lovebugs, a species of march fly found in parts of Central America and along the Gulf Coast. I've seen them even on my way to Disney. I didn't even think it was the season.

These bugs live only four or five days in a state of constant copulation, and in flight can reach altitudes of over a thousand feet. Their favorite pastime is splattering all over windshields.

MAY 12

Unlicensed taxis are on the rise. Why? Is it that the companies' leases are too high? They are. Or is it that business is great? It isn't.

A day doesn't go by that I'm not at the airport, and there he is, a gypsy cab driver, unloading luggage from his trunk, kissing his customer's ass and wishing him something like "Have a nice day." I look at the back of the vehicle, and there's no medallion. Only some homemade sign on the door like "Joe's Cab," or "Affordable Taxi."

These guys have balls. I asked one guy where he was from, and he told me to mind my "own fucking business." This *is* my business! The only thing I can think of is the cab commission we have is so inept people can get away with anything. I mean, every time I get the tag number of a gypsy and report him, nothing happens.

MAY 13

When you work late at night, it seems that convenience stores are unavoidable. Often fares will call from there or flag you down as you go by. Drug runs are another sure thing. We call them round trips, and of course, we often stop for coffee, snacks, that kind of stuff.

The Sunoco at Howard and Morrison is a hub for after-hour revelers and walk-ups. I got a call there at 2 A.M. from "Kashawn," who wanted to go to Lois and Nassau. He owed someone money and needed to pay him and come back to the Sunoco — an excuse common among people out to buy drugs. Another excuse is they need to see their boss or their cousin. The most original one I ever heard was from a guy who claimed to be a process server for men delinquent on child support; he wore wifebeaters and had facial tats.

Kashawn directed me to a white house with a two-car garage, twin palms in the yard, and a pickup truck out front. He went in and out in about thirty seconds. As we were leaving, I noticed another cab pulling onto the block. As I dropped him off back at the gas station, I saw through the open door of a car a nearly naked woman pleasuring a guy. All this out in the open.

About an hour later, I got another call at the same Sunoco, and some guy said he and his wife had a fight, and he wanted to go by her friend's house and see if she was all right. Destination: Cass and Delaware, a known drug hole.

After I returned this loser to the gas station, I got a call on Avenue A just north of Kennedy. Guess where this guy wanted to go? Lois and Nassau. He said he needed to pay back some money he owed his boss.

MAY 14

Thanks to one of our drivers who clued me on the drunk who ripped me off last Saturday night. Addison provided me with the name of his attorney, and I contacted him by phone. I explained to him that I had been the possible victim of a crime. His client owed me money, and I wouldn't prosecute if he paid me what he owed me. Maybe I should press charges, seeing that he was arrested just six weeks ago on a felony theft charge and released on $5,000 bail. He's been arrested sixteen times in the last fifteen years

Surprisingly the guy called me on my cell phone and was apologetic. We've made arrangements for me to pick up my money at his hair salon. Maybe I can get a free haircut.

MAY 15

My taxi blogger friend in San Francisco believes

that unlicensed taxis are a real threat to his business and the general public.

In San Francisco, they have a real problem with former cabbies driving unlicensed cabs with no medallion. They're usually guys who've been fired from various cab companies and still want to drive a taxi. They're losers and the lowest form of life on Earth. All of the lousy cab stories I've ever heard from customers were probably from what a gypsy cab did to them. The tragedy is that in Tampa, the Commissioner of the Tampa Public Transportation Commission allows gypsy-type cabs to flourish.

What he's done is allow more permits to drive cabs than the market can bear. He knows there are enough losers who'll scarf up these permits because they're incapable of doing anything else for a living other than mopping semen off the floor of a local porn shop.

Since these guys do not serve the general public, they hang out at the downtown hotels, cruise ships, and late-night bars. They're what's wrong with the business. It's the commissioner, Sam Lebowitz, who's allowed this to continue. He's only interested in whether a cab needs a wash or not.

MAY 16

My cab, the old 497, was chosen by a production company to be featured in a Publix Commercial. Why they used my cab is unknown to me, but they did pay me for the use of it. They hired an actor to play me even though I was more than ready to be on camera.

They tore the shit out of the trunk to put in a platform so a cameraman could get inside and film a smiling driver loading groceries. That was a million miles away from being real. Most cab drivers hate grocery runs. The people go nowhere; there's a lot of work involved and no tip. They also outfitted the cab to make it look like a stupid checker cab — no idea why.

MAY 17

Fred is the starter at Tampa Airport. The new system funnels all the rides that go out through Mac. He's a good guy, but he's in a position to make or break your day. If you are on his shit list, that's not good. How do you spell Westshore? That's a minimal ride, barely leaving the airport property. Then there's St. Pete Beach. That's where I've been going a lot since this new system was installed. Mac is a friend of mine, and the airport has been my savior recently.

MAY 18

Steve worked for Allied Cab when I first started. He's a good guy and a great mechanic. He's been with the company longer than anyone. The hard work, I believe, has taken its toll. He recently had a stroke.

He's now been released from the hospital and seems to be doing much better. It was a close call, but the doctors believe he should have an excellent recovery and be okay.

He says he's bored hanging around the house, and he wants to come back to work. That should be around September if he continues to make good progress. Hang in there, Steve.

MAY 19

I read a variety of nonfiction books. Information is important to me, and I don't have time for made-up stories when true stories are more compelling. Keep in mind, taxi drivers often have time to read between calls. I have three books on my front seat right now. The Tim Tebow book, *Through My Eyes,* often provokes a response from passengers while Mark Fuhrman's *A Simple Act of Murder,* about the JFK assassination, is of interest only to people of my generation. In the book, Fuhrman destroys the single bullet theory from the angle of a homicide detective. *Cigar City Mafia* is popular with locals who're interested in Tampa's mob past.

MAY 20

This BlackBerry computer dispatch system we use at Allied Cab has some flaws. The software often crashes and drains the batteries fast.

The batteries won't hold a charge for long, and the car chargers stop working after a couple of days. Your only option is to go to the shop and trade your charger for another one.

The weekend is more problematic. The shop is closed, and the women in the office have to charge batteries and look for chargers. You can tell they'd prefer to be doing something else, but they don't have much choice with all the drivers coming in and shift workers complaining that the car they're taking out has a defective BlackBerry.

I decided to resolve the problem myself, so I went to a Best Buy and bought a charger for $12. It works, and I'm back trying to make money. I expect better service from the company than this. As a cab driver, I'm their customer, and I have certain expectations.

MAY 21

A Tampa taxi driver needed an ambulance at the airport. I hate to see this. I got sick at the airport recently, and I hope he's all right because cab drivers have no insurance, and hospitals are expensive. Charles Bukowski wrote in a famous poem about fate, "Dinosauria, We," that we're born into this fate, into this country where it's cheaper to die than pay medical bills, where people plead guilty because they can't afford good lawyers, where the jails are full of crazies who should be in madhouses, where fools become our national heroes.

MAY 22

Too much fast food is the bane of a cabbie's existence. I eat most of my meals from a bag shoved out of a drive-thru window. There are health consequences.

I now have gout, an excruciating form of arthritis. It's caused by an indulgent diet. There may also be a hereditary component.

This time the doc prescribed a new medicine advertised on TV, called ULORIC. It's supposed to dissolve the uric acid crystals in the joints. Gout is associated with high levels of uric acid.

The medicine is costly, and I won't be able to afford it after the two-week free sample is up. It's back to pain for me.

MAY 23

I began driving a cab until something better came along. That's what I told myself. It was addicting, and I stayed with it. The job can be exciting. There's no other like it. One trip can be a business person going to the airport, and the next can be a guy at a convenience store who looks like a serial killer who might've just slaughtered an entire family a block away.

I drive a lot of hours. That's a downside to the job, but the flexibility of being an independent contractor makes up for it. If I want to stop and go to a movie, that's my choice. If I want to sleep in on Monday morning, nobody calls the house, saying, "Where the hell are you?" Nobody.

MAY 24

Lately, drivers have been dropping like flies. I can't count how many dead bodies they've had to pull out of cabs. I'm not going to let that happen to me.

The recession has taken its toll on me. I'm morbidly overweight, have incredibly high blood pressure, and my heart's not doing so well. I'm trying to do something about it, such as swimming for cardio. It may save my life.

I recently started swimming and was barely able to make it to the end of the pool. That's fine. Give me two years, and

I'll lose 90-100 lbs. I bet I'll qualify for the Masters Nationals. I know I will.

If I don't do this, I'll be dead before I'm sixty. Not many options here.

MAY 25

Memorial Day. *The Rush Limbaugh Show* was coming on, so I turned it off. I don't need to listen to him spend the next three hours extolling the virtues of the great health care the United States has, and how wrong the Obama plan for medical insurance is for people in this country.

I don't need to listen to that. I can only tell you I'm fifty-two-years old. I work seven days a week, seventy hours a week to make a living driving this cab. I'm hardly a bum, and I can't afford medical insurance. I can't afford the $800 to $1,000 a month it would take to purchase it as an individual. I have what are called "preexisting conditions." I have high blood pressure, and seven years ago I was admitted to a hospital which wrongly put on the form I was having chest pains. I had an ear infection, which was causing vertigo. There's a clear difference between vertigo and chest pains, but no insurance company will insure me now because they think I'm high risk.

What Rush Limbaugh and Sean Hannity won't tell you is although we have the greatest health care in the world, we don't have access to it. Not all people. It's estimated forty-five to fifty million people don't have insurance. The insurance companies won't insure you if you have preexisting conditions or severely limit whatever coverage would be available and will drop you if you make a claim.

I'm a independent contractor for a company that doesn't provide a group health plan. In fact, fewer and fewer employers in today's world offer group insurance. I did find a company out of Orlando — "Shifting Sands Mutual" or was it "Sinkhole Life and Casualty" — that was willing to offer me a policy which amounted to like a $5-off coupon or 10% off on Tuesday with no prescription coverage.

The only thing that's going to happen with Obama's plan is fifty million people are going to get *insurance*. It's just insurance. No one is going to lose their civil liberties. No one is going to lose their constitutional rights. No one is going to have to live in a state of communism. England has national health care, and they also have civil rights. No one ever lost anything because they got insurance. Yes, Rush Limbaugh, we do have the best medical care in the world, but we have one of the worst insurance systems to the point that the insurance companies are operating a scam.

I pick up people here in Tampa all the time, rich people, take them to the airport, and the fare may run $17 and they give me a twenty and say, "Keep it." I'm supposed to buy my insurance out of that $3 tip. I'm willing to risk my life to take them to the airport, but I'm not good enough to have insurance. Something is wrong. Something is very wrong with this system, and it needs to change.

MAY 26

It's about time! The Tampa Taxi Commission has allowed an overdue rate hike. The standard rates are still the same — two bucks on the drop and $2.25 a mile. What's changed is a fuel surcharge and a new airport flat rate. It's now a $15 minimum for airport service and $25 downtown — to and from.

They're trying to help us with the gas. So we get to do what other businesses do: pass it on to the customer. This new rate helped me the other day when I got a fare at the airport, and he wanted to go to the mall. We can also add $1 on all metered fares for "Emergency Fuel."

MAY 27

As the sun sets on the West Coast of Florida and I head out to make money, I figure this is paradise, what could go wrong? Well, usually, nothing. Often, when things happen, it's the result of the bad behavior of customers.

There's something that happens to people when they get into the back seat of a taxi. It's like road-rage times ten, a frat party gone bad. All common decency, courtesy, and civility go out the window. Drivers are the target, and the effect of this abuse is often unknown to customers.

For example, a fare I picked up at 1 A.M. went to the Crows Nest. There was only a five-dollar charge on the meter, but this guy busted out a fifty-dollar bill and wanted me to break it. I can't give him all my change and let the whole world know I have that kind of money. When I told him I didn't carry that kind of cash, he gave me major attitude.

The next few fares didn't do much better.

Two guys I picked up at The Hyde Park Cafe wouldn't tell me where they wanted to go, only up to Fletcher. Not good enough. I need to know where the hell people are going. His only response was, "It's all good."

The next guy was worse. When he got in at the Tiny Tap, he could only say *Uck ooo at holme*. What the hell does that mean? This guy was shit-faced, and they only serve beer in the joint. He repeated *Uck ooo at holme* another time. It finally dawned on me he was saying: "Fuck you, asshole." We hadn't even left the parking lot yet.

The next drunk would only say, "You know where I'm going. You take me there all the time." I'd never seen this guy before in my fucking life. He finally told me his destination, and on the way kept muttering something followed by, "Know what I mean?" I just kept saying, "Yes." Finally, he screamed, "What the hell do you mean *YES*."

And it was a slow night.

MAY 28

In my years on the job, I've never had anyone compliment me on my clothes. I don't exactly dress like a slob. I shower twice a day, use deodorant and toothpaste. In short, I'm reasonably groomed.

I've always worn polo pullovers. Yesterday I went to Bealls Outlet in Britton Plaza and bought a $10 Florida shirt. It looks like a Hawaiian shirt. A button-up. I've never worn a shirt like this.

My first pickup, a lady at a bar, said, "Nice shirt."

My next pickup was at a gay bar. This would be the real test. A guy got in, told me where he was going, and we started on our way. After a couple of minutes, he said, "Nice shirt." I was elated. My mood quickly turned when he said there was a problem. "What's the problem?" He said he had no money. That *was* a problem. I pulled over to the side of the road and asked him to get out.

He said, "Can I suck your dick?"

It must be the shirt.

Later at the Econo Lodge, a weird-looking dude said he wanted to go to Lazzara Liquors to talk to his old friend. "Nice shirt," he said. I must've reminded him of a bodyguard type. I'm half Italian.

I did have a lousy yuppie experience just before I went home. I had a call in Hyde Park. It took me about three minutes to get there. I responded right as the call came in. When I got there, a car was parked out front, and they were loading their luggage into it. I pulled up and asked them why they even bothered to call a cab. The guy said he tried to cancel. That was a lie. I asked him very politely if he could call and cancel so I wouldn't lose my out. He became hostile, used profanity, threw a five-dollar bill on the front seat of my cab, and stormed off.

It must be the shirt. I've decided to use it as my avatar.

MAY 29

Scores of angry drivers parked their cabs outside Allied Cab's headquarters today. I joined them in a dispute with the company over a new communications system that isn't working and is costing us fares and cash. It turned out to be quite a to-do with newspaper reporters and a television crew. I was interviewed and got to see myself on TV.

A few weeks ago, the company began rolling out a new computer-based dispatch system that involves the use of a dashboard-mounted BlackBerry. Our general manager, Ryan Percy, told the press, "This is much more efficient. The drivers have been asking for this."

The problem is we're not getting the calls we used to get. They might as well have installed a computer virus. The company's plan is for all its cars to have the new communications system, which will work out well for them because customers will be able to swipe their credit cards and receive receipts.

Sounds great, but credit card money goes straight to the company, not to the drivers. They keep it as payment toward our lease.

When I spoke with Ryan, he was kind of pissed. "We have 252 cars," he said. "There are only about fifty or sixty protesting drivers out there. You guys wanna make money or what? You need to stop your whining and start driving."

Later, outside in the parking lot, my friend Ibrahim wasn't happy. "We work so many hours, and we aren't making money," he said.

MAY 30

On the plus side, Allied Cab is also installing modern tablets in their cabs. Our customer service will be vastly superior to Bay Cab. The GPS function is full screen, and the customer can see the driver is taking the most direct route.

I like that the search functions automatically refreshed

when I used it for the first time. It'll also check you in and out of zones as you roll around the city. I don't see much downside to this.

JUNE

JUNE 1

I was leaving the airport today and saw an Allied Cab with the area code for Pinellas County stenciled on both sides. That's our company but licensed for the St. Pete–Clearwater area. The driver looked familiar, so I followed him up Memorial Drive to the Town & Country area. Finally, at a red light, I saw who it was: it was Fish.

He's a driver who's been around forever, but it's been at least ten years since I last saw him. Some longtime drivers may remember him, but most of them are dead.

I honked, and he honked back and waved.

JUNE 2

Last night a cab driver, Jerome Loy, was shot twice in the upper torso during an attempted robbery. Two guys hailed Loy's cab and gave him directions to some shithole apartment complex. A cabbie is making a big mistake picking up flaggers, something I never do. In New York, people hail taxis all the time, but this is Tampa. It's way too dangerous.

Upon arriving at the apartment, one guy got out, and the other stayed in the backseat, pointing a pistol at the driver and demanding money. When Loy refused to hand over the cash, the nice young man shot him twice.

Miraculously, Loy was able to step on the gas, but he didn't get very far, crashing into two transmitter poles and a tree. At that point, the shooter jumped out and started to run, but the fool tripped, losing his shoes and dropping his gun. He picked it up quickly and ran in his socks into an apartment. Witnesses told police where to find him.

"Scooby" Masaka is now being held without bail. The police are still looking for his buddy. As for Loy, he's listed in critical condition at Tampa General Hospital.

JUNE 3

Last night was all about people addicted to the night air, trying to do things they had no business doing: going to leather bars in Ybor City, looking for glory holes in Drew Park, trying to score rock in cheap motels, using cabs to go on fast-food runs — people gotta have their fun. As a cab driver, I'm glad to see passengers, but time spent waiting is a bad deal for the cabbie, especially at a crucial time like 2 A.M. when the bars close. The average wait at a McDonald's is about twenty minutes. I'm not interested in hanging in line, listening to the cab radio as billions of calls hit the board, and I can't do a damn thing except tell the girl, "A #1 with a Dr. Pepper." That's a Big Mac value meal for those who don't frequent these places.

JUNE 4

John Agan was robbed the other night. He's a local Bay Cab driver who used to work for Allied. He experienced the worst thing any driver could go through. He had a gun pointed at him.

Unknown to the robbers, he was on the phone with his wife. He repeated the directions the robbers gave him to let his wife know where he was so she could call the police. He picked these guys up on Fowler after sunset. They eventually beat him, put him in the trunk, and left him for dead. Hours later, someone heard his cries and called the cops. Mr. Agan has now quit the business to which he gave eighteen years of his life.

I drove a cab for two years in Las Vegas in the early '90s and had to go through a security seminar before they'd issue me a hack permit. I still live by what they called the BIG FIVE RULES that drivers should never break.

1) Get a clear and precise destination. Don't put the cab in drive until you know exactly where your fare is going.

2) Get a deposit. If you think the ride is shaky, get money up front. *No dough, no go.*

3) Leave your radio on.

4) *NEVER PICK UP FLAGGERS!* 93% of all cab robberies are from flaggers — without exception young males.

5) Let dispatch know where you picked up and where you're going. That alone could scare off a robber.

Mr. Agan violated at least two of these rules, including the most important: he picked up flaggers. They'll kill your ass.

JUNE 5

I had a pickup at Rocky Creek Mobile Home Park Sunday. This very pleasant older man wanted to go to the bank, then to Sweetbay Supermarket. It was the fifth of the month, and his check had been direct deposited into his account.

He went to the ATM and was having trouble working the machine. I decided to wait and give him a little more time to get his money. Then a real fear set in. What if the deposit never posted? What if he couldn't get his money? What do I do?

Do I leave an older adult at the bank with no money, knowing he couldn't walk back home? What if he got killed crossing the street? I decided to help him. I climbed out of the taxi and went to his aid.

The problem was he didn't understand the touch screen. He grew up in a world where this stuff didn't exist. It was beyond his ability to comprehend. So I helped him get his money, and we were on our way.

I didn't charge him for the ride.

JUNE 6

Cab drivers often get pickups at Tampa General Emergency Room. Late-night people get hurt or sick and have no money to get home, and the hospital pays for their ride. Allied Cab has a billing arrangement with the hospital. Usually, the trips are routine — not tonight.

A woman came out and gave me an address somewhere in Valrico. Our new system has GPS, but for some reason it was frozen, despite my efforts to get it to work. I had no idea where her street was, so I asked her. She called me a "dumb ass" and that I needed to find it myself. She said she was pissed because she had a car parked in the hospital parking lot, and they wouldn't let her drive it.

When I was getting off the Crosstown Expressway onto Faulkenberg Road, I asked her what direction to take, and she started cursing and said, "Don't you *fucking* know?"

I can't speak for most cab drivers, but I've learned over the years not to take this type of abuse. Up ahead was a gas station.

I pulled into the parking lot, a well-lit place, and told her

I needed directions. Through tears she told me how to get to her apartment.

JUNE 7

Things are getting scary. Thugs aren't only robbing cabbies; they're severely injuring or killing them. What can we do?

The latest victim was a terminally ill man, Dwayne Eagan, who was trying to make some money for his wife before he died. Last night, he picked up two young males, and these scumbags sliced his throat from ear to ear, then ran off with Mr. Eagan's money. They were later found by police at a drug house buying $45 worth of crack. Fortunately, they were caught and are now in jail, awaiting trial.

I wish all cabbies lived by the BIG FIVE RULES. They constitute a gospel for all cab drivers. The cabbie last night picked up flaggers. Eagan, who miraculously lived, said these guys looked like trouble, but he failed to get any money from them up front.

I hope this cabbie recovers, and I hope his cancer miraculously disappears.

JUNE 8

My brother Tom took a photograph of me from the parking lot of my apartment complex when I lived in Bradenton and was going to school (I'm 80-100 lbs. heavier now. It's scary what severe depression can do in the long run). I'd forgotten about this image until it showed up on Facebook.

It was the mid-'80s, and I was working for the *Sarasota Herald-Tribune*. That was a fantastic time for a young man in such a beautiful place. The West Coast of Florida has a lot to offer in outdoor activities, and when you're young, you tend to gravitate toward the beach. Why not? There were always girls out there.

Siesta Key was the ultimate hangout with miles of white-sugar sand. You could jog, walk, bike, and ogle girls galore. The water was crystal blue, and swimming was always fun. Europeans would ask me if it was topless. They found it hard to believe Florida didn't have such a thing.

The state did, at one time. Lido Key was a topless beach until the late '70s. The Bible-thumpers protested, and they put a stop to it. That amazed me. Why would an area as cosmopolitan as Sarasota want the rest of the world to think we were a bunch of backwater hicks? After all, tourists bring their money.

I didn't know it at the time my brother snapped the photo, but I'd soon be on my way to Tampa for another newspaper stint, albeit a short one. *The Tampa Tribune* would eventually lay off my department because of downsizing. It was the late '90s, and they were losing circulation, as were all newspapers with the advent of digital media.

Out of a job, I ended up driving a cab for a living.

JUNE 9

Today I used my super-saver card to lower the price per gallon of gas. Every time I buy certain items, such as coffee and food, I get points. Each point is worth a penny a gallon. I had about sixty points.

I need the break on gas because, for the next five weeks I'm driving for Lighthouse for the Blind & Low Vision. The summer program has started for the teenagers who'll get summer jobs. This program is a lifesaver for me financially because it occurs during the slowest time of the year. I've driven for them four years running, and without it, I don't know how I'd survive the summers, which are getting slower every year.

JUNE 10

People who know me know I work the hours of a

pimp. Only the money's not as good. We cab drivers often kid ourselves into thinking we're safe working the "good parts" of town.

Take last night. This dude wearing a black leather jacket got in my cab at the Best Western on Westshore. I checked my clock. It was 4:30 A.M., and the vibe was wrong. He had no luggage and said, "Take me to the bad part of town." What the hell is that? I told him to be a little more specific. He seemed agitated, so I took him across the street to where some other cabbies were hanging out and told him to see if they'd help him. He got out but not before calling me a "cracker motherfucker."

Magnum P.I. always had a saying about going with your little voice. My little voice told me trouble was brewing. My hunch was later confirmed when dispatch said to be on the lookout for a black male with a leather jacket in the Westshore area who'd just robbed a taxi.

I took a call on the causeway (a safe area with high-end hotels). At the Radisson, which is owned by George Steinbrenner, this yuppie-looking dude walked up to my cab. He was wearing dress pants and a tie covered with blood. I locked the doors. I will not under any circumstances transport someone covered in blood. He looked like someone kicked his ass.

The next call was at the Bennigan's Tavern on north Dale Mabry. Two young guys got in and wanted to go to Rome and Spruce. This situation had DRUGS written all over it. The bottom line is they both ran on me, but I didn't want their drug money anyway. One of them left his cell phone on the back seat. Later, his mother called the phone and wanted me to return it. I told her to look in the Hillsborough River across from the art museum. Happy swimming!

JUNE 11

There's a tropical formation between Cuba and Mexico that's producing needed rain for drought-stricken Florida. The benefits are excellent, but it could cause problems.

We get busy when it rains. However, that isn't always good. Tampa's roads flood quickly, and many of the calls we get are on impassable roads. The water can quickly flood an engine, which means it'll be ruined and will have to be replaced.

If I flood an engine, I just bought it. I always say *Don't drown, turn around.* A little rain can help business, but torrents can wipe us out. It's early in the summer, and it seems like we're going to have an active hurricane season.

JUNE 12

I worked the entire night last night and not once went to Ybor City. There's a reason for that. Ybor is a violent, crime-ridden area that isn't safe, and it's the bar owners' fault.

When I first came to Tampa, I was impressed with the Cuban and Latin history of this neighborhood. It was once the cigar capital of the world and is now an arts district. In the mid-'90s, it had the potential to be the new New Orleans. Located close to downtown and with the ability to line one restaurant or nightclub side by side — why not?

This concept worked for many years as this was *the* spot to go and was worked by at least a hundred different cab drivers, almost exclusively on the night shift. Now many of them, including me, go nowhere near the place. The reason is crime — violent crime.

For some stupid reason, the owners of the clubs didn't follow the New Orleans model. They didn't go after people with money to spend; they went after the under-twenty-one crowd. Why? I was that age once and didn't have a nickel to my name. How can you make money off people who have no money? A recent Google search of "Ybor City Crime" yielded countless hits. A friend of mine took his wife to Muvico

Starlight 20 Theater the other night and left around 9 P.M. and were robbed in the parking lot by a young man wearing a do-rag. Is this where anyone would want to drive a cab? I refuse.

The *St. Petersburg Times* interviewed the manager of a nightclub about crime in Ybor when a fight broke out in the background! It was captured in a photo that ran in the paper.

Too bad this enormous potential has been wasted.

JUNE 13

The Weather Channel says the tropical storm that's been threatening the coast is being upgraded to a hurricane. That means many streets on the south side of Tampa will flood, making them impassable.

Visibility is poor, and that's why I'm now home, waiting for this to pass. Allied Cab doesn't care. I still have to pay my stand dues. I'll definitely come out on the short end of the stick on this deal.

Fox News is now saying a private plane crashed into a house about fifty feet from the runway at Peter O. Knight Airfield on Davis Island. Why is someone flying in these conditions? I know why. In my thirty years in Florida, I can't count how many false alarms and nonevents we've had. People begin to ignore warnings after a while.

JUNE 14

On the old STAND 21 in Hyde Park, I saw a little kitty and his littermate. Someone dropped them and took off. That's mean. They were very friendly and social, perfect kitties for adoption. There was a food bowl next to a tree, so people were feeding them. A cab driver friend of mine, Roger Billings, said he was going to go by and check them out. Roger likes cats and takes in strays. He's worried now since his neighbor has been killing his cats. He called the cops and got the runaround.

JUNE 15

This morning, I picked up these guys at the Mons Venus and they made a couple of stops, including the Shell station at the corner of Kennedy and Howard. That's when the problem started.

They tried to pay for some beer with a debit card which was declined. They came back to the cab and referred to the clerk as an "asshole," saying they lived only a couple blocks away and would walk home. They tried to use the debit card to pay me. I said no way. I needed cash. I was now the asshole.

I picked up the phone to call the cops, but they were gone.

JUNE 16

I got a "Corner Call" — a call at a street intersection, not an address. It turned out to be a gaunt young woman wearing a hoodie. It was about 100° outside.

She opened the back window and hung a cigarette out. "You can't smoke," I told her."

"I just got out of the emergency room," she said.

I looked at her hand holding the cigarette. A white bandage showed under the sleeve. I looked at her face, which was thin and ashen.

"Got knocked down and robbed," she said. They took everything. Except my phone."

Here we go again, I thought, another waste of time. "So how are you going to pay?" I asked.

She said her brother would pay on arrival. I told her I needed some assurance of that. She said I could have her shoes.

I stopped the cab.

"Lady, I can't help you. I'm not working for fun."

She refused to get out, then pleaded with me to take her to the cops. "They'll give me a lift," she said.

Hoping to calm her down, I suggested she call her brother and have him wait for us. She raised her phone, put it to her ear, and immediately started talking, seemingly before any connection.

I pulled into a mall parking lot, got out, and opened the passenger door.

After a minute, she climbed out, and mumbled into the phone, "The cabbie's an asshole."

She wandered across the parking lot, still mumbling into the phone. I cleared the meter and left.

JUNE 17

When you're living in a state of semi-homelessness, you have trade-offs. I pay the cab company $92 a day six days a week and have to buy the gas, and I don't always have money. I haven't had the $4.50-a-load to wash my clothes.

Some drivers opt to eat Vienna sausage, Ramen Noodles, dog food, and so forth. I use my laundry money to buy better food (pasta with Ragu) and generic prescription drugs for blood pressure. Thus, my dirty laundry gets recycled.

A fellow cab driver told me candidly my shorts were so dirty they looked like I'd shit in them. He said I also smelled terrible. The customers must've noticed too, so I had to use some of my rent money to do laundry, shorting the manager of the hotel where I live.

JUNE 18

I picked up a lady from Puerto Rico at the La Quinta hotel near the airport. She'd moved to Florida to work in the cleaning business. She'd contacted a woman online about being a supervisor for her company. The offer sounded good, so she moved her family to Tampa. This is another reason to be careful about Internet contacts. When she got to Tampa, the woman wouldn't answer her calls. All the lady had was an address in Tampa Heights. I took her there, but it was a private residence. The people who lived there knew nothing about it.

The poor lady started freaking out and sobbing like crazy. I decided to see what I could do to help her.

In the front seat of the cab, I had *The Tampa Tribune*, Sunday edition. I gave her the classifieds and assured her the demand for people with her experience was huge in this area. I told her that if she followed through on the help wanted ads, she'd have twenty jobs come Monday. Besides, Tampa is a great place to live, despite her initial experience. As for her $106-a-night hotel, I took her to a more affordable lodge — $40 a night on Kennedy Boulevard. I know where all the low-rent places are. I live in one.

She couldn't have thanked me enough. This is just one of many things we cab drivers do for distressed and displaced people. We're the true social workers. By the time the world has kicked them to the curb, we come by and pick them up.

JUNE 19

In all my years of driving, I've never been at fault in an accident. Today I was. My foot slipped off the brake, and I rear-ended the car in front of me. Fortunately, nobody was injured. Slamming into another car traumatized me because I've never been in this situation before. Others have hit me, but I've never hit anyone else.

JUNE 20

It's not the dog days of summer yet, but it might as well be. I had a call today midtown, and this lady wanted me to take her dog to PetSmart so he could make his pedicure appointment. The bug exterminator showed up just as I arrived, and she was afraid he'd steal something out of her house and wanted me to take the dog to PetSmart. So I loaded Buddy and took off. He sat in the backseat and watched traffic go by. We're not allowed to transport unaccompanied children, but there's no company policy about unaccompanied dogs.

Buddy turned out to be a good ride. At least he didn't complain about me taking him the wrong way, and I could play the radio without him telling me to change the channel. He was one of the best-behaved fares I ever had.

I took him inside on his leash and waited while they took care of him. On the way home, he climbed on my lap and watched the traffic. I stopped at a convenience store, and when I came out, he was looking out the window, wondering where I'd been. I've never had a dog, but I know how people can get attached to them.

When I got Buddy back home, the lady paid the fare in cash along with a generous tip.

JUNE 21

I have a coffee can with my life savings in it. This morning my first fare used a credit card, and I needed gas. I had no cash. So I went home and raided the coffee can and took out the eight dollars I was going to retire on.

Things picked up, and I got some hospital charges that paid two days of my lease. I also picked up a charter that put a hundred bucks in my pocket. Today was a good day. When I was on my way home, I saw a piece of paper blowing in the road. It looked like money! I jumped out in traffic and ran toward it. "Please be a hundred," I kept saying. It turned out to be a twenty. People were blowing their horns.

"Are you crazy" someone yelled.

I got back in the cab and took a picture of it. It'll go in the coffee can, and my net worth is 2.5 times greater than this morning. It was a good day.

JUNE 22

I got burned on a credit card last night. I believe it was a complete scam. This is why cab drivers, drug dealers, strippers, and abortion clinics are reluctant to take plastic, preferring cash. The reason is that we provide an irrevocable service; once it's done, it can't be undone.

The other night I responded to a call in a Spanish-style neighborhood. This young man and woman came out of the house. She got in the backseat, and he came to my window. They said she needed to go to Saint Petersburg, and all she had was $15. He said he wanted to use his credit card to pay the fare. She was going to Brighton Bay Apartments across from Derby Lane. They're nice apartments, but something didn't seem right. I was more than a little suspicious of the whole thing.

I was reluctant because they were young, and their English was marginal at best. Language was an issue because I was having difficulty understanding what they said, asking them to repeat everything multiple times, but I compounded the situation by making a rookie error: *I didn't get approval*. Often it's a pain in the ass to swipe the card, call the number, enter the info, wait for an approval code. I could already be on my way to another call.

As I pulled into the apartments, she grabbed the door handle; and before I stopped, she was out the door and into the darkness. I knew the card would be no good. When I called it in, the system said to "pick up" the card, which means it was stolen or reported lost. The fare ran $39.90.

I'll never be beat like that again.

JUNE 23

Many of my friends are cab drivers. I guess that's normal for any profession. You spend so much time doing something that the people you work with become your friends.

One thing that bothers me, however, is they don't want to do much of anything. I know we work a lot of hours, but rarely has a driver offered to go fishing, golfing, bowling, swimming at the beach, or hiking or camping. (Stupidly, I turned down Pirate's request to camp at Hillsborough State Park last year. I regret that.) Nor has any driver taken me up on the offer to do such things. Tammy was the only exception.

Many of my cabbie friends have dropped dead — heart attacks, cancer, you name it. Sitting on your ass and smoking three packs a day isn't the healthiest lifestyle.

JUNE 24

People with bank accounts and credit cards may wonder what Amscot is. Amscot provides financial services to people who don't have traditional relationships with banks.

Why do I know this, and why is it important? Many of my fares have fallen between the cracks and use Amscot, as do I.

Banks don't want these people. Society may not want them either, but they represent a growing underclass in Tampa that votes and one day may have their voices heard.

The current mayor isn't their friend and has done nothing to solve the housing problem in this city. I drive all over town, and all I ever see is economic activity designed to make the rich richer.

I've always believed every dime in the pocket of the poor will find its way into the pocket of the rich.

JUNE 25

Allison and Sampson showed up at my place for an impromptu party. Sampson was a soap opera star in Ethiopia, and Allison is a former cab driver from London. She recently quit the taxicab business and now paints houses for a living. We drank beers and laughed and had a good time.

JUNE 26

The new function on the tablet lets the driver request a call-out. I use this only at night. During the day, I knock on the door.

I tapped the horn at an address on a dark street. There were no lights on inside, and I wondered what kind of call this was. Were they going to the airport? Were they drunk? I got out of the taxi and knocked on the door, nobody answered.

I got back in the cab and requested a call-out. Billy called and said the customers didn't see me outside the house. Strange. Why didn't they answer the door? I knocked again.

From the porch, I could see the street sign at the corner of the lot. I walked over to it and realized I was on the wrong street — an excellent way to get shot. It's happened before.

One time I could see people screwing in a back bedroom while I was looking through the window. The woman glanced up, and I know she saw me (I was at the wrong house), and I got out of there fast. They may have seen my taxi speed away.

JUNE 27

There was a time when taxi dispatchers mattered. They were the pitchers on a baseball team. Piss them off, and you'll strike out all night. If they liked you, it was nine innings of home runs. Now, with the GPS system, dispatchers are marginal players. All they do is answer questions and make address corrections. I liked the old days because our reliable customers got covered, but I'm adapting to the new way.

JUNE 28

We were headed down the interstate towards downtown when she started talking on her cell phone. She was arguing more than anything. People who live marginal lives exhibit a lot of frustration and poor communication skills. Even after many years of driving a hack, I've never gotten used to crappy people. I find it amazing how fares will talk about their personal lives in front of a total stranger. We're invisible; we don't exist; we're nobody.

We pulled up to the Greyhound Bus Station, and there

was nowhere to park. The front spots reserved for taxis are always full. The bus station is on Cass Street, which used to be a cable car street back in the day. It also has train tracks running down the middle headed for the dock area. I was left with no choice but to double-park and pop the trunk.

This is the point when the fare will usually pay, or get out and help unload the luggage. Instead, she took off and went inside the bus terminal. That left me with the task of unloading her stuff onto the sidewalk. Much of it was in boxes, and many items were loose. She had hairdryers, makeup cases, all kinds of stuff.

It took me about ten minutes to unload all of it, and she still hadn't come out. I now had to find her. That meant I had to leave my taxi in the street and all her belongings on the curb. I wasn't comfortable with that.

I started walking to the front door when I spotted one of the "cabbie cops" from the Tampa Transportation Authority. He was looking for the driver of the cab double-parked out front.

That, of course, was me. He demanded to see my hack permit and my drivers license and started yelling at me about leaving my cab on the street and blocking traffic. I tried to explain to him the circumstances, but he'd have none of it. The fact that there was no room to park meant nothing to him. I asked him if he wanted customers inconvenienced by parking on the side and having to schlep their stuff around to the front.

He said he had a better idea: park on the railroad tracks in the middle of the street. Right, pal. The only people these guys bother to police are taxi drivers, but they wear Rambo gear and carry sidearms, all in the service of shaking down guys like me who're just trying to make a living. He had me sign a $75 ticket, which stated I had two weeks to pay it. The Tampa Transportation Authority prides itself on not taking any taxpayer money to survive. They do it all on the fees they charge drivers.

While all this was going on, the woman finally got her stuff off the sidewalk. I got back in my cab, angry that I now had a long way to go to make up for this stupid ticket.

JUNE 29

I dropped off a fare at an upscale office complex near Reno and Cypress and then parked near the beach. I don't think I'd ever been there before.

After a nap, I strode by the dunes, walking past them and onto the beach. It was a beautiful summer day, still early enough in the year that it wasn't too hot. I did notice some guys out fishing. The beach isn't in the best shape. There's a lot of seaweed and trash. It's also loud here. The park is on a direct flight path to the airport, and planes fly overhead all day long, only a few hundred feet above.

JUNE 30

So ends the month and with it the smell of dollar bills, or is it an illusion? Maybe not.

We were swamped today. Since the 4th of July is on a Saturday, many people are taking next week off, and they're getting out of town early. I hope this'll continue through Monday. I need the money. I'm getting ready for an excellent 4th with a cookout, beer, and firecrackers.

JULY

JULY 1

I make it a point to work the airport as holidays approach because I can get cash fares, mostly from recreational travelers who have real money, and I need money. The $113 trip to Hudson, I didn't turn down even though the lady said she was going to use a credit card.

As I've already made clear, the problem with credit cards is I can't cash them out. When the economy went south, I ended up $1,400 in the hole. I've now beaten that down to $72; but when you're in a hole, they won't cash you out. In other words, they keep it and apply it to the books. The result is I often don't have money for gas or food. It's not a great way to live, but I'm close to putting this recession behind me and getting on with my life, something I've been trying to do for a few years now. Maybe some hope and change will come my way.

My computer died; my TV died; my stereo died; my digital camera was stolen. My phone is all I have. I hope to get a laptop when I get out of debt.

Anyway, it was a beautiful day at the beach. I wish I could've gone swimming.

JULY 2

Today was the first time since 2007 that I didn't owe Allied Cab money. I paid off the balance today and got cash back!!! At this pace, I should be able to buy a new laptop soon and write from the comfort of my home, instead of trying to write in a crowded library with the librarian in the green shirt (the same shirt he's had on for weeks) sitting across from me and chewing his tongue while making funny noises.

I had a time call this morning at one of the new condo developments that are ruining South Tampa (affordable housing is vanishing). I was right on time, and the lady had a pile of luggage and was going to the airport. I crammed her stuff in the trunk of the cab, and we took off.

When I turned left onto Gandy, she started yelling, "Where are you going?"

"You're going to the airport, right?"

She said she was but she wanted to pick up her boyfriend first at Post Hyde Park Apartments. She thought I knew that.

"How would I know that?"

"I called last night and told them where I was going."

She thought I was a smart-ass when I told her they didn't give me her itinerary.

She got on her cell phone while I turned right on Bay to Bay. I was planning on taking Palm over to Howard via Isabella. The shortest distance between two points is a straight line, but when I turned onto Palm, she said, "You're taking the scenic route."

I pulled the cab over to the side of the road and told her we weren't moving until she stopped making accusations.

I finally got her to where she wanted to go.

JULY 3

"What's the breaking point?" That's what a cab driver said to me at a Citgo gas station this morning as we were filling up.

He said he was new, and the cost of gas was kicking his ass. I could feel his pain since I now pay about $70–100 more a week for gas than I did last year.

He spotted me when I went over to take a picture of the PAY AT THE PUMP sign.

"You're that blogger dude." He said he'd seen my blog when he was doing a Google search for downtown Tampa art.

I wished him well and told him to hang in there.

Thirty years ago Jimmy Carter got run out of town when gas hit $1.19 a gallon. Food for thought.

JULY 4

There's a mural on the side of a building downtown. It incorporates some of the iconic images of Tampa's history. I'm amazed at all the newcomers who know little about the area's history. For example, Plant Hall was the logistics and command center for the Spanish American War. Teddy Roosevelt was in command. As a result, the Rough Rider Krewe is still essential to Tampa culture

It's hot on this Independence Day, and so is the taxi business. Activity at the airport is way up with little wait time. The streets are full of calls. It hasn't been like this since 2007. If I make it through this summer, I'll be in the clear and finally get my life back.

JULY 5

The laundromat at 2708 W. Kennedy Boulevard closed the other day — just another sign of how upscale Kennedy Boulevard is becoming. The working poor used this laundry. People like me. No more. High-end condos are replacing affordable housing in South Tampa and Hyde Park and are now encroaching into West Tampa. Businesses that serve the needy and the poor are vanishing.

When I started driving a cab in '95, there were two prominent laundromats in Hyde Park: one on Kennedy and one at the corner of Platt and Howard, which is now a mortgage broker's office. I was a friend of the owner, Bob, who said a week didn't go by without someone coming in and making him an offer for the property. The prospective buyers had no intention of keeping the laundromat. Bob finally got an offer he couldn't refuse and sold.

As a result, I started doing my laundry at the location on Kennedy and often talked to the lady who'd owned and run the place for years. One day, she told me her business wasn't doing well. She said she couldn't afford the required maintenance. Last time I was in there, almost all the machines were busted and the soap dispensers had no soap.

Now I know why. She was planning on closing and had lost interest in it. What happens now? Where do renters go to do their clothes. Not everyone lives in a $400,000 condo. I live in a shithole motel room — more evidence of the vanishing middle class when guys like me work their ass off and can't get ahead.

I was there today taking pictures when a car pulled up with laundry in the back. A guy got out and read the sign in the window. He looked disgusted and left.

JULY 6

I work with special needs children at Lighthouse for

the Blind & Low Vision. Every summer, they have their transitional training program, which teaches them adult skills and how to take care of themselves. Tonight, we had the awards dinner, and it was fun.

The ladies all received flowers, and I got a certificate (the kids call me *Mr. Tim*). In the photograph I took, the young lady in the foreground is only fourteen, blind, and has a better attitude about life than most adults. She doesn't know it, but she's my hero.

JULY 7

I had a recent trip to Polk county out of the airport and swung by the old family house on Sandpiper Lane in Mulberry. I didn't stay long. The sight of others living there wasn't good. So I left.

My father was an engineer who designed nuclear-powered submarines. He got a job working for General Dynamics in Tampa after working twenty-five years for Newport News Shipbuilding. The family followed my parents down to Florida, but in a piecemeal fashion.

My sister, Mary Lou, was living in West Virginia at the time and didn't make the move. My older brother, Mike, was already living there with my parents, whom he would continue to live with the rest of their lives. My twin brother, Tom, moved down to attend Florida Southern College. He now has a happy and prosperous life with his wife, Sandy, out in California. Our dog, Norman, was also there, one cool little dog. We had him for fifteen years before we had to put him down. My sister passed away in '83, and our parents are now gone.

Today, I just wanted to stop in front of the house where at one time I was nineteen-years-old and was just beginning to figure out life.

The first thing I noticed was that the present owners had torn out all the trees and parked two pickup trucks in the front yard. I couldn't believe it. Those trees were beautiful, and it was like living in the woods because we were so surrounded by them. Oh well, it's their property. They can do what they want, but it used to be ours. It was like something sacrilegious had happened.

JULY 8

Since this is the era of hope and change, I have some hopes of my own. I hope the economy is getting better and things are finally improving. I hope I'll soon get a new laptop and get back to serious photo editing and blog posting. Time is marching on; Tim is marching on; the meter is running.

I started blogging in 2005 during the heady days of the Tampa blog scene. It was new and fun, and I couldn't wait to get home and write about my daily trips. Something changed along the way, however. The United States economy stopped working, like a three-dollar watch, killing hope and breaking the spirit of many. Most of the local bloggers just went away, their sites left abandoned years ago, proof of a once vital community killed off by economic realities and a quickly evolving social media culture.

My blog description ("Daily thoughts and inspirations from a Tampa taxi driver on the back half of life") is more important to me now then just stories about drunks and strippers.

In the coming years, I may get out of the cab business, develop different interests, or pick up new hobbies. Moving out of Tampa is an option. One thing will never change — the meter will always be running.

JULY 9

Starting next year, drivers picking up passengers at Tampa International Airport won't have to compete with taxicabs for space at the curb.

The airport is going to ban commercial vehicles from going

into the baggage claim area. "The biggest traffic problem we have at the arrivals curb is all the taxicabs," said Louis Miller, executive director of the agency that runs the airport. He believes that taxis "jockey" for position and block outside lanes and stop traffic.

As a professional driver who's never engaged in such behavior, I find that statement insulting. Most divers are courteous and play by the rules. The problem is that older people and those unfamiliar with the airport layout are blocking lanes.

Miller (who didn't return my calls) thinks he can state generalities and broad suppositions about people. He even said some vans park at the curb for two hours waiting for fares, which is something I've never seen.

JULY 10

I got a call at a grocery store. Most cab drivers don't like grocery calls. The reason is simple: they don't go far and they don't tip. I have to get out of the air-conditioned cab and load their groceries, rarely with any help. All in all, grocery runs are a pain.

As I got out, I saw a lady and two small children, three or four years old. That meant they needed car seats. Cab drivers don't carry car seats. We need the space in the trunk, and it's the parents' responsibility to have them.

I informed her that I couldn't carry her, and she became hostile. One of her kids was in the car, and when I got in, I told her she had to leave. When the girl got out, she went to close the door, and her mother screeched, *"NO! LET THAT FUCKIN' CRACKER CLOSE HIS OWN DAMN DOOR!"*

That hurt.

I read in this morning's paper that there was a funeral in Detroit to bury the "N" word. That's great. I don't use the word although I hear it a lot living in racist Florida. Considering the way whites have mistreated blacks over the centuries, maybe black folks could've coined a stronger pejorative for whites than just *cracker*.

JULY 11

Longtime driver Justin was in a terrible accident the other night.

He trained me when I started in the taxi business and became a fast friend. When I first met him, he said: "Don't let anybody tell you driving a cab is a stupid job. That isn't so. To be a good cab driver, to be a successful cab driver, you've got to be sharp. The successful ones are some of the smartest people I know. You have to be."

I fear he's not going to make it. A tree fell across the road and crushed his cab. He was cut out of the taxi and is now in a coma, hooked up to a ventilator. He's now technically brain dead and isn't responding.

What's ironic is that he smoked and drank and never really took care of himself. Justin is 73 years old! I guess Cary Grant was right: if he knew he was going to live this long, he'd have taken better care of himself.

That's about all I know. We can only hope for the best.

The back office is taking up a collection for him. When Justin dispatched, he always collected money for sick cab drivers. So it's about time we return the favor.

I took a picture of Justin at his birthday party at Outback Steakhouse. It was one of the best birthday parties ever.

Hang in there, Justin. We're pulling for you, you grouchy old man.

JULY 12

Picnic Island remains one of Tampa's hidden treasures. I went there today to relax, swim, and get some sun. I wore my thong (just kidding!). The water was still a little too cold for my taste, so I waded around and splashed myself.

At the very south end of the island, there's a hiking trail that cuts through mangrove shrubs. It was ebb tide when I was there, so I hiked out to the east end of the island, where many of the fishermen and crabbers like to go. I don't know what's there that can't be caught on the other side of the island, but there were plenty of people out there fishing.

JULY 13

The dog days of summer are not just hot in Florida, they're rainy, altogether monsoonal. At least they used to be. I've lived in Florida for thirty years and have always been amazed at the intensity of afternoon thunderstorms. Florida is the lightning capital of the United States. (No coincidence that Tampa's NHL team is called The Lightning.) Lately, however, thunderstorms have been as rare as hen's teeth.

We're getting clouds, but no rain. I have no idea what's going on. I'd've thought with global warming, it would be storming every day, and we'd have floods like Houston. Or maybe it's just climate change in general. Humans have certainly done their best to destroy the earth's environment.

JULY 14

Cab driver Lina Faison was found slain near Azalea Middle School. Someone going for a walk near the school discovered her body. Police later found her abandoned cab in South Pasadena. It's believed she picked up a customer at 5 A.M. That's all the police are saying.

JULY 15

I was leaving Port Tampa this morning when a tanker truck pulled right out in front of me. He then proceeded to go about twenty miles an hour up Interbay towards Dale Mabry.

I tried to pass (on the double yellow) and made it as far

as his driver-side door when oncoming traffic forced me back behind him. So I tried to pass again, up parallel with the driver, who was looking at me, and then back behind him. This went on all the way up Interbay.

I must've scared the driver, who probably thought I was a lunatic or a madman and was determined to get us all killed. I just needed to get to my next fare. I snapped a photo of the truck with my cell phone at the light at Dale Mabry. He was turning left just like me. I needed to get this guy out of my life. So when the light turned green I took the inside route and sped by him. I was not sure but he seemed to be flipping me off. It must've been a reflection in the window.

JULY 16

I picked up two beautiful young women this morning at a Westshore hotel. Their destination was an address up in Carrollwood. For some reason, I thought they were hookers. I was right.

Hookers have gone high tech. One of them had perfect directions to their john's house. She was reading them to me off her iPhone. I guess business must be good for her to afford one, but she did lament all the "cancellations" they get.

After I returned to town, I got a call at the DoubleTree on the Courtney Campbell Causeway. It was a time call, so I stopped for gas on the way. I arrived on time, passing a Bay Cab coming out. Shit! That asshole took my fare. Billy, our night dispatcher, believes Bay Cab is scanning our calls to make up for their lack of business. I then got a call at the Hyatt on the Causeway. When I rolled in, a Bay Cab was pulling in. I beat him to the punch and picked up. He drove by slowly. I think Billy is right.

Another lady at the Econo Lodge wanted to go to Carrollwood to pick up her grandson, of whom she had legal custody. When we got there, she went to get him, and the other grandmother came out. They were arguing over the boy, each with a different interpretation of the court order. The other grandmother finally surrendered the kid after about twenty minutes of arguing, but she said if the kid wasn't back by next Saturday, she'd call the police.

I hate getting in the middle of shit like this. The lady was on her way back to Dallas with the boy. I told her to contact her lawyer when she could and let him take care of it. Child custody disputes put people through living hell.

JULY 17

Life as a hack is a unique experience. There's no other profession like it. Drivers who're attracted to it are usually free spirits and mavericks with a sense of cowboy independence — a fancy way of saying *anti-social*.

On occasion the money can be okay, but to earn even "okay money" I must be willing to operate outside the boundaries of what's considered normal. By that, I mean working late and early morning hours, weekends, working the bars and strip clubs. We're on the front line of social evolution. If you want to see the future of America, look in the back seat of a cab.

That's why this job isn't for everyone. When I started doing this years ago, I quickly understood that people don't always call you under ideal conditions. Often there's a problem in their life, and that's why they're calling. They'll call us before they call a cop, a priest, a social worker, an ambulance, AAA, or a moving van. We're not in any of these businesses, but people think they can talk us into it.

Mostly it's the circumstances alone that put them in a weird situation. Take this morning, for instance. I got a call in the wee hours to an establishment in Drew Park called Fantasy Land. The manager needed a cab, and I had to wait a few minutes for him to come out.

While I was waiting, a guy walked up to the cab and wanted to know if I was hip?

"Hip?"

"You know, are you with it?"

I didn't know if this is a setup or what, and then it dawned on me he was soliciting me for gay sex. Several places in Drew Park are known as cruiser joints.

I told him, "You're not my type."

He seemed disappointed.

JULY 18

I took a passenger way out to the Turkey Creek area, then went to a beautiful park for a couple of hours. As Tony Soprano said: "Sometimes you just gotta smell the gorilla shit."

This boardwalk is next to a camping area and goes out to a wilderness preserve. There's an observation tower which gives a spectacular view of a former phosphate mine, but there's nothing natural about this area. Engineers are responsible for the lakes, not nature. There was a storm brewing in the distance, and I could hear thunder. So I cut the trip short. I barely made it back to the cab before the rain hit. We had a dry few weeks in early July, but now it's been raining every day, and we're not in the rainy season yet. Wait until a hurricane strikes.

JULY 19

Two cab drivers in Saint Petersburg were killed in the last three days, and nine have been robbed since April. What is this? The killing fields? Cabbies are scared.

JULY 20

Today I drove to the Myakka River State Park. Besides being one of my favorite places, there was a Bigfoot sighting there recently. I wanted to check it out. The video

I uploaded to YouTube shows the observation tower in the background. From the top of the tower the entire park is visible in a 360-degree panorama. I always make it a point to climb to the top of it.

From the base of the structure, a nature photographer captured an image of a Bigfoot in the area where I'm standing in the video. It's normally dry through here, but unfortunately we've had a tremendous amount of rain, and it does look like something has been moving through here, sloshing through it.

Unfortunately, this area right now doesn't look like a good place to research. That water has risen to about a good half a foot to a foot deep, enough to prevent me from getting through there.

The Myakka River is on the other side of the tree line. For any team coming in here to do Bigfoot research, it's going to be a bust unless they like wading in hip-deep mud. The golden rule of Bigfoot: do your homework. Florida has a long rainy season, which makes Bigfoot hunting difficult from May through October.

I decided to head out to the savanna where a recent team found prints and a primitive structure. Actually it's been almost two years now, so a lot can change. I suspected that the savanna was underwater, and it was. I didn't bring my waders, and quite frankly, I just wasn't in the mood for it.

JULY 21

I've seen this lady for years pushing a cart down the street, loaded with bulging garbage bags. She's mentally ill. You'd think someone would help her. The police could Baker-Act her and get her help, but the cops won't do anything. They say it's a liberty issue and she can do what she wants. Funny, when it comes to everything else, law enforcement is all up in everybody's grill.

JULY 22

Edgar called today. He needed a designated driver to the Rays vs. Red Sox game. Ticket included.

It was only the second time I'd attended a Rays game, and what impressed me today was how many people were cheering for the Red Sox.

I find it hard to believe people who live in this area, own homes, have businesses, kids in school etc., cannot cheer for the local team. People are moving to the Tampa Bay area, and they're having babies down here. Aren't those kids going to be fans?

I won a bet from a man whose family I was taking to the airport who said he didn't know anyone who was born in Florida. I asked him where his children sitting in the back seat wearing Red Sox gear were born. You got it. Tampa. That's my point. He was trying to do what the man was doing who was sitting behind us at the game. He had his little 4-year-old boy decked out in Red Sox gear and was telling him all about Fenway Park, telling him all the old stories and singing the Red Sox fight song.

JULY 23

Trying to develop regular exercise habits is difficult. My favorite exercise is long-distance hiking, which is brutal in the summer heat and humidity. The pool now seems like the place to be — wear swim trunks, get a tan, have fun.

Along the coast, the crowds are teeming, and there are signs of expansion. Many of the mom-and-pop properties were razed to make way for condos, most of the demolition taking place in 2006, just before the economic collapse. In Clearwater today, I spotted several tower cranes in the distance, something I haven't seen in years. It must mean the economy is recovering.

JULY 24

Melissa Plaut is a New York cab driver who's as tough as any man. She's also a gifted writer who started a taxi blog in 2005 called *New York Hack*. She began chronicling her adventures in cab driving in the Big Apple and soon caught the attention of the national media. Her story will soon be released in book form.

She writes in an amusing and witty style. She cut her teeth on writing ad copy for a Manhattan firm. After being laid off from her job, she had to pay the rent and so began driving a hack.

She uses rough language and pulls no punches letting people know what cabbies go through, everything from drunks to her fear of being robbed.

What she does discover and eventually writes about is the sub-culture of cab driving and how the occupation eventually seems like a fate in which you are forever trapped. After the denial and deal making stages, cab driving becomes a matter of acceptance, ultimately leading to self-fulfillment and redemption — a way of grieving for our past life and the knowledge that this is all there is and we've found our place. We can now be happy.

Unlike me, she always stays on topic. She rarely gives her political opinions or talks about sports. I guess she figures who gives a shit. That's a lesson I could learn. Her blog was so good, the news media wanted to interview her. She was interviewed on ABC news, and that put her on the map big time. As she would say, she has "major balls" doing this for a living.

JULY 25

Allied Cab got a toll violation from the State of Florida. Their cameras took a photo of the tag of a taxi not paying the toll and sent it to the company. The low-resolution image made it difficult to read the cab number, and they thought it was me. Impossible. I never use the toll roads.

We're only talking about $3.50. I went in to contest it, and sure enough, the tag number didn't match mine. I'm 378, but it was 338. I was off the hook.

Allied Cab doesn't like getting these things from irresponsible drivers and charges a $25 handling fee. They're in the cab business, not the toll business. I was ready to pay, but I'm glad it wasn't me — just an oversight.

JULY 26

It's bad enough that it's slow out here, but why do I have to get my chops busted as well? I think some people expect way too much and are mean.

I had a pickup at 10 A.M. going to the airport. I was there on time; I loaded the luggage in the trunk. My cab was immaculate as always.

Within five seconds the lady was on her BlackBerry.

At the airport, she pulled out her checkbook and wanted to write me a check. I told her I take only cash. She then whipped out a credit card, and I told her I didn't take those either. She then said she knew the owner of my company and would create big trouble for me. Fine, I told her, call the owner. I spelled my name for her. In the end, I took her plastic because I had no choice.

JULY 27

People who read my blog know I was a philosophy major. The *St. Petersburg Times* had a brief write-up about me in their BLOGWATCH section today: "Tim Fasano is a Tampa cabbie with a few things to say — apparently more than he can share during a typical fare. So he launched *Tampa Taxi Shots,* a blog that includes photos he shot of the city and some of his Allied Cab friends. 'I'm a philosophy major who is searching to see if Bertrand Russell was right about man being a rational animal. Not yet found one.'"

I've always been quite interested in the philosophy of Bertrand Russell despite one regrettable yet understandable fact.

During the Cuban missile crisis, Russell sent a telegram to the Soviet leader, Nikita Khrushchev, appealing to him not to be provoked by the United States' "unjustifiable naval blockade of Cuba." He told Khrushchev he admired the way he'd acted with "magnanimity and grandeur."

Just to be clear, Khrushchev said history was on the side of the Soviet Union; and speaking about the West, specifically the United States, he said, "We will bury you!" Everyone took that to mean nuclear annihilation.

History was not on the side of the Soviet Union. Whether it will be on the side of Bertrand Russell is hard to say. When he died in 1970, he was far better known as an antiwar crusader than as a mathematician or philosopher. Nonetheless, his contribution to philosophy will be remembered.

JULY 28

About three years ago, a group of malcontents who'd been fired by Allied Cab sued the company and Marjorie. They retained a Harbor Island law firm to take the case under some labor law that said independent contractors should receive the minimum wage.

I'm not sure of the disposition of the case, but I think Allied Cab paid them money to go away. That's the problem. They didn't go away. They started their own cab company. It's called Tampa Bay Taxi. The problem we've had with them is they're jamming our stands. Allied Cab divides the city into sections, and we have arbitrary stands where we sit waiting for calls. Drivers from this company have been sitting on our stands, taking up all the shade to make us suffer. If they're looking for shade, they could park elsewhere.

I asked one of their drivers if he could be professional enough to find somewhere else. He gave me attitude. So I called the manager of their company and explained the situation to him in a professional way. He said, "You got some fucking balls telling my guys where they can sit."

JULY 29

Sunday mornings I see these guys (some gals) at major intersections, selling the Sunday paper.

Most of them are homeless, but they have a chance to make up to $75 for their efforts. It's honest work, and who're they hurting? How it works is they pay 25¢ for each paper and sell them for one buck. Sell a hundred, and you make $75. Not bad.

The Saint Petersburg police consider this panhandling, and therefore a crime. Know what? Sometimes the cops can piss up a rope.

Many of these poor folks have interesting stories and seem very motivated. I always buy from them when I can, chatting with them on occasion. I want to help, but I don't always have the spare change.

JULY 30

It was a late night, and I got what we call a "Corner Call" — a call at a street intersection, not an address. All I know is that it was someone named "Mark."

That makes the call a higher security threat. The best calls have a name, address, and phone number.

I picked up this early-twenties-looking guy and found out where he was going. Then I started making conversation.

There's a reason I want to talk to my fares. Of course, I like to be helpful, but I'm also looking for information to qualify the individual without getting into their business. If I get details, then I feel safer and more secure about the ride.

Plus, it's more likely I'll be paid. People who're up to something get very vague.

A golden rule of cab driving is to get a clear and precise destination. I got that, and we were on our way.

"Mark" told me he left his apartment because he had a fight with his girlfriend, whom he described as a *psycho bitch*. He said she drank all the time and constantly argued and wanted to fight. I hear this kind of thing a lot. People always want to make the other person out as responsible for a bad situation.

"What's going on in your life?" I asked.

"I just told you. My girlfriend is fucking crazy."

"Do you have any hobbies or activities you enjoy?"

He now sounded annoyed. "Dude, I just told you my girl is fucked up."

I tried to get him to figure out why this messed-up situation seemed so attractive to him. People don't keep going round and round with each other because the sex is hot or they're lonely.

The most challenging thing is to take a hard look at yourself. When things fall apart in your life, you have to try to figure out what you did to contribute to the situation. Blaming someone else is easier.

"What do you do when you're not with her?" I asked him.

He said he hung out with his friends. They'd go down to Ybor and hang out. It seemed he just kind of hung out.

That's the problem with being young — you don't always have a clear sense of identity, which can lead to severe feelings of insecurity and poor self-esteem. Separation from someone else is at the root of "Mark's" anxiety. He's clinging to her to fulfill what he lacks in himself. I know the feeling; I've been there.

I was forty-years-old before I began to develop a real sense of identity and could recognize the things that gave meaning to my life. Growing up can be a bitch, and in my case, it was a long, lonely, and painful process. I wouldn't want to be his age again, facing that kind of learning curve. No way.

I dropped him off at his friend's house. The lights were still on.

He told me he was afraid his chick would come looking for him. I doubt that was what he was afraid of. The sad truth is he's years from understanding that.

JULY 31

The only reason I'm in line on the red side at the airport is that I was told about 60,000 Shriners from all over the world were coming to town. Where are they?

I don't expect a lack of business when a major convention is in town, but that's what we're looking at. Not one call from a Shriner. It looks like the Shriners used the courtesy vans, hotel shuttles, Super Shuttle, and Tampa Shuttle — but not Allied Cab.

Lucky for me, I picked up a family who wanted to go to the gulf beaches, and I got $60 for the ride.

AUGUST

AUGUST 1

I wanted to start getting some exercise today. Jimmy Connors once said that the best exercise is the one you'll do — that's why I went lap swimming in a pool in Saint Petersburg. Too bad I couldn't do that so easily in Tampa.

Tampa keeps cutting back on pool services and, as a result, fewer people use the pools, and the city continues cutting back. That's not what they do in St. Pete, which has the North Shore Aquatic Complex with two of the biggest swim teams in the county. The St. Pete Masters Swim Team is the best in America. Nothing like this is going on in Tampa. I read today Tampa is scaling back the Bobby Hicks Pool.

Why? It's a long-course pool, which is in high demand. Tampa doesn't get it.

I've always loved swimming, a sport I competed in when I was a teenager. My high school yearbook in 1973 had a few words to say about my swimming:

"Mark Spitz, look out! Swimming in competition since the age of twelve, sophomore Tim Fasano earned a gold medal in the State Junior Olympics held this year in Charlottesville. He finished fourth in the 100-yard breaststroke and swam breaststroke on the winning medley relay team. The medley team, composed of local peninsula swimmers, set a new state record of 1:47.5."

AUGUST 2

I lost a friend today. The older you get, the more you have to say goodbye to people. I've been saying goodbye a lot lately.

Justin was more than just a cab driver. He was a gambler and world traveler. He lived a life many people only dream about. Justin never played it safe.

In Texas hold 'em, he was one of the best. He had ice water in his veins, and you could never read his mind.

Kate was a friend of his. He called her "Tex" for her husky voice and cowboy hat. He told her I was gay, and she should leave me for him.

Life is brief. Justin is just another I'll see on the other side one day.

AUGUST 3

I'm usually up to see the sunrise. It's a peaceful time of the day. I'm feeling fresh, sipping coffee, and welcoming the new day. That, however, is sometimes ruined by a frequent experience with fast food joints.

Take McDonald's. They claim that 53% of their business

is breakfast and most of that goes out the drive-thru window. Then why do I have so many problems with it?

The girl will always fold the bag so I can't see what's inside. I start driving down the road, headed for a call, reach into the bag, and items are missing. Why? Aren't most orders combos? Sandwich, potato, drink. What could be so hard about that?

AUGUST 4

Elizabeth from the *St. Petersburg Times* called me today. After getting home to the awesome aroma of pot roast cooking in my crock-pot (a gift from my sister-in-law), my cell phone rang. She saw my posting on the Shriners, and the newspaper was going to do an article in Friday's paper about conventions and their economic impact in the community.

I emphasized to her that the Shriners are a fabulous organization that builds hospitals for sick children, and not one parent has ever paid a dime for their child to be in a Shriners Hospital. However, their frugality did us cab drivers no good. They didn't use our cabs. We need groups in here that'll spend money.

She understood and promised me the headline wouldn't read "Cab Driver Slams Shriners."

AUGUST 5

I have a defective tire rim. I got gas at the Shell at Kennedy and Howard and noticed my hubcap was missing — third day in a row. The shop replaced it twice, and this morning it was gone again.

After they replaced it the first time, I was going down Kennedy, and I looked in my rearview mirror and saw the hubcap rolling across lanes of traffic and cars almost crashing, trying to avoid it. The Tampa Public Transportation Commission can issue a $20 fine for not having a hubcap.

I picked up a middle-aged guy this morning at the Crosstown Inn at the corner of Gandy and Dale Mabry. He told me he'd spent the last four hours trying to buy crack and wanted to know if I knew where he could score some.

The next pick-up was a stripper who wanted to know if she could smoke her weed. No, I told her. *Mind if I smoke?* It has a whole new meaning.

AUGUST 6

I don't know who's sponsoring this event, but every Sunday on the east side of downtown, there's a feeding station for the homeless. If the cab business doesn't get better soon, I'll be in that line.

AUGUST 7

I was quoted in the *St. Petersburg Times* in the article about the Tampa Convention Center and all the different types of conventions held there:

"'Perhaps the Shriners were too well-behaved,' said cab driver Tim Fasano, who also writes the *Tampa Taxi Shots* blog. He didn't see a single fare from a Shriner. 'Let's face it, it's a bunch of old men who go to bed early. For us, it was a flop.'"

Later in the article: "Fasano, the cabbie and blogger, recalled that the best was a gay and lesbian convention about 10 years ago. 'They went everywhere,' he said. 'They were so determined to show the city how much (economic) impact they have, they stamped their money. I got a lot of gay money. You know, it spends as well as straight money.'"

AUGUST 8

Things haven't been good. I'm okay, but the cab business isn't. I guess business is down in all fields, but it's especially hard in the transportation industry.

It looks like my prediction came true: that despite how

bad things got, none of the immigrant drivers would give up. They keep putting in their fourteen-hour days, seven days a week and somehow think life is good with their $200 a week (about $3–$4 an hour). They must not have anything else to do — no kids in school, no hobbies, no fishing buddies. They never plan for weekends at the lake or sporting events. They never think of swimming at the pool, or going to the gym, or hanging out at Borders for the afternoon. They drive their taxi as if that was all there was. I can't win against this kind of mindset.

Many of them are homeless. Just go to the holding area at the airport in the middle of the night, and you'll see at least a dozen taxi drivers sleeping in their cabs.

I've been very depressed and have had no energy to write. I've never felt like this before. There's been a lot going on: Obama's visit to St. Pete, police brutality in Tampa, cab robberies and murders in Tampa, but I don't have the energy to give a shit about any of it.

I've decided to stop feeling sorry for myself and somehow try to improve my life, but I don't know how I'm going to do that. I can't make a living anymore.

AUGUST 9

My retired cab-driver friend Larry read with interest an article published in yesterday's newspaper. It was about a seventeen-year-old girl named Sarah who died from an overdose of drugs and alcohol.

How was an underage girl allowed to drink at a night club? Sarah was wasted when she and her friend wrecked their car in Riverview, and sheriff's deputies let her go without calling her parents. A few hours later, her eyes rolled back into her head, and her breathing stopped, and not one of her friends who saw her dying called 911.

What bothered Larry and me was the way the deputies handled it. I won't transport a minor, especially one who's wasted. Cab drivers see drugged-out people all the time. They're common on the outskirts of downtown and in crime-riddled neighborhoods. These are people who've hit rock bottom and beyond, usually the result of a long skid into their own hell. Sometimes jail saves them or an intervention from what few friends they have left. They aren't usually from the suburbs. Sarah was. Sarah didn't have to die like this. Forget about her friends. Other areas of society failed her in a criminal way.

The two culprits were Ybor City and law enforcement. If Ybor City had become the new New Orleans, as it was highly touted to be years ago, they would've been catering to a decidedly adult audience with money to spend. As a cab driver, I stopped working Ybor years ago because the bars were catering to young people with no money, some underage. Then the gangs moved in looking for trouble. And I mean trouble. People started getting killed.

AUGUST 10

I went to my doctor today because I wasn't feeling well. He sent me to Tampa General because of extremely high blood pressure (212/110).

I drove to the shop and had a driver friend of mine give me a ride. When you have paperwork from a doctor, they take you right in, and there's no waiting for hours. I was glad for that.

They administered an IV drip, and they got it down to 130/70.

A hot LPN hooked me up. I thought my nurse fantasy might come true after all — but not today.

After an afternoon in the hospital, I'm home and feeling better. I need some significant lifestyle changes.

AUGUST 11

Joe is a mechanic in our shop. The shop boys work hard in the heat to keep our taxis running. Joe is one cool dude. He's always in a good mood and will pick you up if you're feeling down. He's always excited about things and has countless ideas to make money — like today.

I came by the shop after I was done for the day to pay my weekly lease, and Joe came out, saying he had something to sell on eBay. He asked me to snap some photos of a vintage bicycle.

He had the bike in the shop. I told him to position the bike just inside the shade. Bikes aren't my specialty. He said it was a fifty-six-year-old English Racer, and he wanted a couple grand for it. I hope he gets it. It just looked like an old bike to me.

AUGUST 12

It looks like a giant storm is headed our way. In fact, the Weather Channel has a projected bull's-eye on the Tampa Bay area.

Most people in Florida have not lived here long enough to realize there's been a lull in Hurricane activity since 1973. A lot fewer people lived down here then. According to my insurance lady, the great migration of baby boomers came between 1973 and 2003. These boomers have no idea what's in store for them. Keep in mind it was hurricanes that stopped the land speculation in Florida during the 1920s, not the Great Depression.

AUGUST 13

One bad thing about sitting on your ass all day is you gain weight. Look how convenient all the drive-thrus are. I'm no stranger to them. Burgers, fries, chicken, tacos, gyros — cab drivers consume massive amounts of this stuff.

I've gained a lot of weight since I started driving a cab. The only way I've ever been able to control it is by working out in the gym and swimming.

AUGUST 14

While I was waiting outside a house early this morning before sunrise, I noticed this incredible moon. I took out my camera and using the window jam of the front door, snapped a wonderful shot. I could see craters and mountains. I wondered if lovers actually do gaze at the moon and express their hopes and dreams. I never have. The moon doesn't seem all that interesting.

I read recently that the concept of love has changed over the last 2,000 years. The Romans believed Cupid with his arrows made people go insane in a way like nothing else.

The only Shakespeare I can quote is from *Pericles*: Antiochus points to skeletons held up by a wall and states:

Here they stand martyrs, slain in Cupid's wars;
And with dead cheeks advise thee to desist
For going on death's net, whom none resist.

You don't have to read this obscure play to know what the Bard is talking about. Man will always be drawn to love like a moth to a flame.

Breaking my reverie, my fare showed up with his suitcases. I hit the meter, and we were off to the airport. Another ride, another $20.

I'd take love over anything else that's out there.

AUGUST 15

Roland Casanova is an expert on almost anything dealing with modern life, art, entertainment, magic, *Star Trek*, movies, horror shows, and pop culture. He works the late shift at the 7-Eleven at Gandy and MacDill. A few years ago he was the host of a public access television show called *The World of Roland*. I met him by accident.

No matter the subject, he knows it. You can walk in and mention a scene in any movie or *Star Trek* episode, and Roland will know it. I once asked him how the magician David Blaine levitates surrounded by a crowd. Roland said he does it by "exploiting technology and devices unavailable to yesterday's generation." Then he turned his back to me and proceeded to *RISE OFF THE FLOOR ABOUT 6 INCHES!!!* No way it could've been a trick. Noland said it was. He then showed me how to do it. I promised to keep his secret.

AUGUST 16

Another one of our drivers passed away yesterday, found dead in his room.

Ramon was one of several drivers who've passed away in the last six months, and I put the blame squarely on the economy which has forced guys to work sixteen hours a day, seven days a week, for very little money. We're talking about guys in their 50s and 60s who just don't have it physically to do this job, which will beat you into the ground. In this line of work, you never get the rest you need.

And I continue to see ads saying: *Be your own boss. Get paid daily. Make $500 a day driving a cab.* It's like a siren song.

Desperate people with a dream swell the ranks of drivers so much that nobody can make any money. Oh, and the conservative talk-show hosts want you to vote for politicians who're going to cut the taxes for the wealthiest people in our society, and hopefully one day that money might trickle down into my pocket. I'm still waiting.

AUGUST 17

When I get to this house, they have their luggage stacked on the porch. They had about thirty pieces of luggage. Most of them were duffel bags as big as golf bags. How they thought I could get all that stuff in my cab is beyond me. There were also four adults to fill up the seats.

I told them I couldn't help them, and they got pissed. They were now going to be late for their flight, and it was my fault. I told the guy I was going to try to get other cabs over to help, but he said, "Fuck it."

At this point, I told him I was no longer interested in helping them. I got in my cab, and when I was backing out of the driveway, I could see they were having trouble getting their shit into their two SUVs. What were they thinking? Probably that I was an asshole.

Later, I picked up this lady from New York at the airport, and she wanted to go to Bradenton. The only estimate she wanted was time. I told her it would take about fifty minutes to get there. She got in but was so busy on her BlackBerry, she didn't notice we were crossing the Skyway Bridge. When we got to Manatee County, she looked up, saw the meter already at $107, and started freaking out.

"How the hell is the meter that high? We've only been in the cab for twenty minutes."

We'd been driving for forty-seven minutes. When we got to her destination, she paid the fare but acted like I'd held a gun to her head.

Later in the day after driving this guy all over Tampa, he gave me a fifty-dollar bill for a $35 fare. When I gave him his change in one-dollar bills (he didn't tip) he accused me of shortchanging him by a buck. I told him that was bullshit and to get out of my cab.

AUGUST 18

"I'm cold. Please turn the air down," she said after stumbling to my cab and almost falling as she opened the door. One thing cab drivers look for are signs that things will go smoothly and we'll be paid. A bad sign is when fares start complaining before they even tell you where they're going.

Bad experiences are typical for cab drivers, as familiar as swamp water to a Florida hog hunter. As much as you trek through it and hope you've reached the end, stretching to the horizon and beyond is the swamp, with no hog in sight. It becomes the norm after a while. We deal with humans; we're not hauling packages.

I turned the air down, and she began to tell me where she was going. I realized she'd not only been drinking — she was bombed. She struggled not to slur her words, saying she wanted to go to the corner of Azalea and Horatio.

Considering where I picked her up, that would be a breeze. Just shoot down Henderson and hang a right on Horatio, and we're there. The start to my night may not be as bad as I thought — no such luck. I hung a left on Henderson, and she wanted to know where I was going.

"You want to go to 3000 Horatio, right?"

"You're going the wrong fucking way."

She thought we should be going south when north is the only way to get there. I tried to calm her down by saying she'd had a little too much to drink and leave the driving to me.

"Drinking? What makes you think I've been drinking?" She slurred her words in a barely audible tone.

"Oh, nothing," I said.

I was trying to humor her, hoping to get her home before she puked.

No chance. She wouldn't leave it alone.

"You're going the wrong fucking way."

She was hostile.

"You cab drivers are all the same. You only want to take people the wrong way and jack up the fare. I demand you turn around."

I turned the cab around. We'd head in her direction, and

I'd take her where she wanted to go, the way she wanted to go there. I didn't care if we ended up in the next county. It would be her way. She remained quiet, and we kept moving along. We now rolled up to the red light at Gandy and Manhattan. We sat there, and she looked around. One thing late-night drivers worry about is that the fare will fall asleep or pass out, and we won't be able to wake them. At least she was cognizant.

"Where the fuck are we?" she nearly screamed. "We're down on Gandy. What the fuck?"

"Ma'am, if you were listening to me from the start, you'd be home now, safe and sound. Just be quiet and let me take you home."

Miraculously, she agreed. I turned the car around and headed north in the right direction. Finally, we pulled into her driveway, a total waste or twenty-five minutes for a ten dollar fare.

The meter said $26, but there was no way she was going to pay it. She was starting to freak at the price.

"Don't worry about it. Just pay me ten bucks. That's what it would've been."

I was trying to be a gentleman about this. You know what they say about no good deed. She got out of the car and threw a ten spot through the window.

"Asshole," she said, walking off into the night.

AUGUST 19

The taxi I'm driving has over 300,000 miles on it. That's usually when most cabs are nothing but a bucket of bolts, but our shop tries to get even more mileage out of them. The shop changes the oil every month and does whatever repairs are needed. Apparently, the front office believes these cabs will run for eternity.

The fare I picked up said she could smell oil burning.

After I dropped her off, I checked the oil, and I could see I needed at least a quart. Considering the oil was changed last week, that meant I was burning a lot of oil. In the fourteen years I've been with Allied, I've never had a new cab, never requested one.

I see other drivers with new cabs, so why not me? I need to ask Syd because I'd like to have a new taxi by autumn.

AUGUST 20

Florida executed another man today: John Richard Marek, who received the death penalty for the murder of Adella Marie Simmons. The victim and a female friend were driving home from a vacation when their car broke down on the Florida Turnpike near Jupiter. Marek and his buddy, Raymond Wigley, offered to take Simmons to a service station while her friend waited in the car. Instead they took her to a desolate beach sixty miles away where Marek repeatedly raped her before killing her. Wigley is serving a life sentence for his role. Where does such evil come from?

AUGUST 21

I had a rough night. I must've set a record for no-shows. What I'm so pissed about is that between 3 A.M. and 5 A.M., I picked up no fares at all. I rolled all over Southside, and not one damn person was home when I got there. Nobody bothered to call and cancel. They just wasted my time. They probably think all cab drivers are scum.

AUGUST 22

Tips are essential to cab drivers' survival. The difference between a good day and an ordinary day is tips. There are situations when we don't receive tips when we should. I had an experience Sunday that demonstrates why people should tip the cab driver.

I picked up this family from Detroit at the Homestead Villa Hotel on West Hillsborough Ave. They wanted to go to Golden Corral for breakfast. When they didn't answer the horn or door, I went to the front desk and waited ten minutes for the desk clerk to finish with a customer. She then called the room and let them know I was there. I went to the room, waited again, and then took them to the restaurant for $3.80. They gave me a $5 bill and asked for their change. They said they wanted me to pick them up in an hour and take them to the cruise port to get on the Carnival Liner. Yeah, right.

An hour later, I was out of the area and heard their call hanging on the radio. I turned it off.

AUGUST 23

Today there was a solar eclipse, but all I thought about was an eclipse from my childhood. It was 1970, and they called it "The Eclipse of the Century." I remember how excited my twin brother and I were to see and capture on 8mm film a total eclipse of the sun. At that age, I didn't know how fortunate I was. I'd learn later that in life we're almost always more fortunate than we think — not something my thirteen-year-old brain could fathom at the time.

I was young, strong, and thought life would last forever. Now I'm an old man on heart medicine. If there's a lesson in all this: don't live life vicariously. Live in the moment. Grab life by the balls. Take advantage of what you have today. Like eclipses, there may not be a next time.

Most of the neighborhoods in Newport News, Virginia, were recently developed to provide housing for the exploding military industry that the Tidewater area was known for. They had that prefabricated look. Most homeowners were of the WWII generation, and their kids were baby boomers.

I miss those times. Society and culture had more continuity. I'm not sure over the decades we've improved much.

Most people valued family and security. It was a great time to grow up. A few months earlier, we watched man first walk on the moon — now this celestial event. Life seemed boundless; the possibilities, endless.

Tom and I had a telescope, and my most vivid memory is going out on cold winter nights and gazing up at the display of the cosmos. There was less light pollution back then, and the night sky appeared vast. *Star Trek* had only recently been canceled from primetime TV, and it seemed that type of future was possible. Our father showed us one night the trail of a satellite as it made its way across the night sky. We looked with amazement and wonder.

With the technology of the times, I did a decent job of filming the eclipse with our grandfather's old Kodak 8mm camera. My father helped me attach a welder's glass to a cereal box. The camera was inside the box. (Unfortunately, the film vanished years ago.) Everything went right that day, including the weather. It was a late winter day, temperature in the 60s. It felt good and got even colder during totality. I remember the diamond ring (Baily's beads) on lunar contact.

Then just like that — it was gone.

AUGUST 24

Many people come to Florida for a fresh start. They'll tell you it's due to the weather, but it usually involves the circumstances of their lives. Things will be better in Florida. They're confident of that. They come here with Florida dreams.

I got a call around sunset to pick up a middle-aged couple living out of a cheap motel. They had Michigan tags on their car. They were trying to survive until they saved enough money for an apartment. Currently, they were paying out the nose for this dump. They needed me to help them with their belongings. They'd filled their car with stuff but had a TV and other items to put in my cab, along with a cute little dog. The lady said it was just too expensive to stay where they were.

I know how they feel. One reason I drive a cab is I can't work at near minimum wage and survive although I pretty much do anyway. I helped them but could see they had a tough road ahead. Low wages and few benefits — those are the jobs in Florida. It was once said you got paid in sunshine. These people found out that sunshine doesn't pay the rent. I hope they make it, but not everyone does down here. The well-paying industrial jobs of the Midwest are gone. That's why so many people from Ohio, Michigan, and Wisconsin head south. People do go back north, but to what?

AUGUST 25

What a cab driver will do to make a living is beyond what most people are willing to do. One thing we do is go into bad neighborhoods and pretend things are normal. Like the Pakistani store owner who sells smokes, beer, lotto tickets, and Phillies Blunts Cigars to people who walk in his door while all the time hoping he doesn't get shot — you begin to think this is normal.

I got a call about 4 A.M., and things got a little weird — not too bad, but not what I was expecting.

It was the Downtowner Motel, one of Tampa's "swankier" joints. It's the kind of place that has weekly rentals and calls them apartments. The guy was on the balcony and very anxious to get going, a clear sign that someone wants to buy drugs. I guess his buzz wore off, and he needed another fix. He and some woman with sunken cheeks and a glazed stare got in the backseat.

After we drove around for ten minutes, we ended up at another fleabag motel, where a black dude on a bike did a "fly-by" of the cab, trying to determine if he had a customer. My fare told me the black dude was a friend to whom he owed money.

I told him, "Get out and do whatever you need to do outside my cab." He climbed out, and after about one minute, returned looking happy.

What bothers me about these people is they think they're slick although they're not fooling anyone. Eventually, cab drivers will stop responding to their calls, but in today's climate and with the need to make money, many drivers take their calls. It's incredible how desperate a cabbie can get for a twenty-dollar bill.

AUGUST 26

I often go to Hillsborough River State Park because of the magnificent sunrises I like to photograph. I don't just shoot the sky. I look for a foreground image that can lead into the picture.

I always use the example set by the great Ansel Adams. When he photographed any landscape, he was on the scene before sunrise. That's when you have great light, colors, and no harsh shadows — especially crucial for Florida landscapes. In the photo I took this morning, the tree line in silhouette almost looks like a mountain range in the distance. That's necessary here because we have no elevation in the Sunshine State. The highest point in Florida is Britton Hill in Walton County at 345 feet above sea level.

AUGUST 27

This morning I got a call around 5 A.M. at the Waffle House at I-275 and Westshore Boulevard, and things went south fast.

This swaying drunk couple came out and wanted to go to the MacDill and Bay-to-Bay area. The Waffle House parking lot is virtually connected to the entry ramp to I-275, so I pulled onto the freeway and took off for Lois Avenue.

After I hit the interstate, the woman said I was taking

them the long way. She then started arguing with me and said she'd lived in Tampa for five years and knew her way around. Before she could finish, I began to turn left onto Kennedy, and she screamed, "Why are you turning left on MacDill?"

MacDill? I let her know we were nowhere near MacDill. Now she was convinced I was taking them the wrong way. I have very little patience for drunks who accuse me of long-routing them.

I pulled into a gas station.

"Get out," I said.

"What?" she said

"Get out."

She said they were friends of Marjorie, our office manager, and I'd just lost my job.

"Tell her I said hello."

They got out and slammed the doors.

AUGUST 28

Pirate, a longtime taxi dispatcher and driver, passed away from natural causes. He was an afternoon dispatcher when I started and was the best voice guy ever. He treated everyone fairly and would never give you a choice call even if you were his best friend.

He did a lot in his life. Fast living was no stranger to him. He lived all over the country and experienced much. He told Marjorie the night before he died that he could go in peace because he'd done everything in life he ever wanted to. Few people can say that.

AUGUST 29

Meet Eloy. He may not look exactly like Hemingway, but he is a real-life Conch. Eloy was born and raised on Key West. He is laid back, sails a boat, slacks off whenever possible, and lives the Florida lifestyle most people are too busy working to enjoy.

Eloy claims there's a saying in Key West: "Don't do today what you can put off till tomorrow." That sounds like good advice to me.

He is just one of the many interesting and unique characters who drive a taxi for a living. I posted a picture of him in his cab to my blog today.

AUGUST 30

I need a vacation. If I had the money, I'd fly to Arizona, a state I've visited a few times. I love the dry desert air out west, which is such a welcome relief from the horrid humidity of Florida. The desert vistas and saguaro cacti are beautiful. Maybe I can scrape some cash together by October when the weather has cooled.

AUGUST 31

Big Mike goes back to the glory days of cab driving in Tampa. He worked for over twenty years with Allied Cab, but when new management took over, he moved to Bay Cab. He wasn't making any money and was trying to survive.

Mike was in the holding area at Tampa airport when I saw him this morning. We talked about how lean it is now and how expensive the taxi leases are. They're high, and the company gets most of what we book. He started driving for Allied in 1983 and has never seen it this bad. His beard had gone completely gray, and his thick glasses kept slipping down the bridge of his nose. He'd aged fast the past few years.

What's sad is so many grown-ass men are willing to do this for meager wages, me included. Very sad.

SEPTEMBER

SEPTEMBER 1

I was dropping some late-night party people off on the west side of the Ybor strip, and I turned down a side street. The sun was up, and I could feel it was going to be another hot day. Over in a parking lot, I could see them. There they were, dozens of them, the chickens! They must've been meeting there to plan the day's mischief.

My fare said he'd never seen hens in Ybor City before. Well, there were several hens with little chicks following. It's right at sunrise that you have the best chance of seeing them. They do seem to be growing in population.

SEPTEMBER 2

I read on Facebook about the death of a former classmate of mine. He'd already lived an entire life, and it seems just yesterday he was a kid sitting next to me in my 10th-grade History class. He became a public bus driver in Newport News, got married, had kids and grandkids, retired — he did just about everything he wanted to do in life, then passed away. And here I am still trying to figure it all out.

SEPTEMBER 3

When taxi drivers drop off at the Seminole Hard Rock Casino, they get a $10 Shell gas card. I finally got a ride there since the promotion started and went straight to the gas station. It helped, and I wish more businesses would appreciate what we do. There used to be more perks in this industry. For example, the company provided a monthly hot breakfast and box lunch, but that was years ago.

SEPTEMBER 4

For the second time this year I was rear-ended. I stopped for an ambulance today and a car slammed into the car behind me, knocking a lady's sedan into my cab. The driver who rear-ended her left the scene, but I got his tag number. The cops later found the dumbass at his house and charged him with leaving the scene of an accident.

There was no real damage to my cab, and I was soon on my way. The long-wheelbase Crown Victoria sedan is one tough car. I understand why cab companies and police departments favor them.

SEPTEMBER 5

In the years I've been driving a taxi for Allied, I've always been a 24-hour driver. I'd like to switch to a 12-hour shift. The reason is easy to explain: when you're a 24-hour or weekly driver, you're married to the cab. Every day I wake up, I'm on the hook for the lease. I'm tired of that. What happens is that years go by, and I realize I've yet to take a day off. Life is slipping by.

With a 12-hour shift, I could work when I want, set my own schedule, and not be married to the cab. When I pay my stand dues at the end of my shift, I won't be committed to another day behind the wheel. I hope I can do this.

SEPTEMBER 6

Cab drivers eat most of their meals in the cab. That's why seagulls have us figured out. Whenever I stop to eat, I draw a crowd. Drivers feed them, and the birds know they can beg and we'll feel sorry for them and toss them part of a cheese burger or a french fry. Seagulls love french fries. I think they must've been taxi drivers in a past life because they act like us. When we toss out some chow, it's a veritable feeding frenzy outside the window — behavior similar to what happens to cab drivers when the dispatcher "flags" an order and it's the first cab there that gets it. We look like seagulls.

SEPTEMBER 7

Labor Day. Not a lot of traffic in downtown. Many people are going to the beach, camping in national parks, and enjoying backyard cookouts.

As I was cruising downtown, all I could see were $400,000 condos under construction. I'm sure the average slave wage earner in Florida can afford one of those. Big deal that Tampa Ship pays $12 an hour, a wage I earned thirty years ago as a welder at the Newport News Shipyard. Welders were members of the AFLCIO — no such unions in Florida. The owners have it all coming their way. The working man not only gets screwed, he supports the very system that does the screwing.

SEPTEMBER 8

I hate holiday weekends. It's slow, no money, and the office and shop are closed. My AC is on the fritz and nobody was around to fix it. In all these years I've never broken down when the shop was open — a massive dose of Murphy's Law.

Now it's raining like hell, AC barely alive, windows fogging up. The good thing is it's the first business day after a holiday. We should be busy. Plus, at the airport, we're on the side that moves. It needs to be busy this week. Let's hope.

SEPTEMBER 9

My twin brother, Tom, posted some pictures of Sandy opening up her birthday presents today. Sandy is one of the few people on earth I would trust implicitly. Love you, Sandy. I hope you enjoyed the gifts.

SEPTEMBER 10

Two guys got in my cab about 4 A.M. at a local hotel. They wanted to go to a Japanese health spa. These places are known as "Jack Shacks." Apparently, there's a happy ending at the end of the massage.

What these two guys didn't know was these establishments are closed at this hour. They close at 2 A.M. Every weekend I pick up guys who don't know this, and I take them spa to spa and act surprised the places are closed.

Tonight I was honest and told the guys that the places were closed. They said okay and got out of my taxi and gave me nothing. A tip for my honesty would've been nice.

SEPTEMBER 11

I drove a guy to the emergency room at Tampa General, but he could come up with only half the fare — a crumpled dollar bill and a baggie full of change. He said his girlfriend was having an emergency and wanted to know if he could mail a check for the balance to the company. I said sure, why not? In all my years of driving, only one person has ever mailed in the fare.

Oftentimes people get in the cab, knowing they don't have enough for the fare. Like the guy last week who picked up two strippers and brought them back to the Marriott and was later out in the middle of the night looking to score drugs. I drove him all over West Tampa. Even the drug boys were asleep at this hour. When I finally got him back to the hotel, he could come up with only $12 on a $36 fare.

SEPTEMBER 12

I'm tired. After working all weekend, I managed to squeeze in a camping trip. I needed a mental break and set up camp in a place that's basically under water because of summer rains.

I found a dryer site, sprayed on OFF, and cooked over a campfire. The area looks like a possible Bigfoot site, so I'll be back out there, maybe in November when the weather is cooler. I did enjoy myself and stargazed before falling asleep. When I awoke, it was my birthday.

SEPTEMBER 13

I'm fifty-three years old today, and I can still bench 300 pounds, not too shabby for a guy my age. The problem is there are mornings when like Rocky Balboa I need a taxi to get from my bed to the bathroom. It's just a matter of taking my gout medicine.

Kate called to wish me a happy birthday and a beautiful day. She called when I was listening to Larry singing "Happy Birthday" on voicemail.

I took the day off, and in the evening thoroughly enjoyed a great dinner: sirloin steak, shrimp, stuffed shells with tomato sauce, and salad.

SEPTEMBER 14

I picked up a woman this morning at the airport. Her daughter is a student at the University of Tampa. It seems her daughter is sick. She has flu-like symptoms, isn't eating, and is throwing up. I told her it sounded like homesickness. She agreed.

Most of the students at the university are from the northeast. I don't know why local students don't attend, but that's the way it is.

Her daughter is young and learning that in life many things that seem wonderful and exciting on the surface often don't meet your expectations. Relationships, jobs, vacations, nothing is immune to the bitter taste of experience.

I told the lady when she said they were from Boston that it must be a beautiful place. She agreed and said Tampa was too.

SEPTEMBER 15

I just finished swimming laps at the Bobby Hicks Pool when I spotted a guy dressed in a Spider-Man outfit go into the lifeguard office. I went over there to check it out. Spider-Man brandished what looked like a 9mm pistol and pointed it at me. The lifeguards were wide-eyed with fear.

I dived into the pool. When I surfaced, he was still in the office, so I climbed out and ran through the back gate and over to the Boys and Girls Club next door. I called the police. I had no idea if he was shooting people at this point.

Within minutes he emerged into the parking lot and got in his car. A cop blocked him with an SUV cruiser and ordered him to get out and hold up his hands. The cops had their guns out, ready to shoot. The suspect complied.

It turned out the gun was a realistic-looking BB gun. He said it was just a joke.

The cops cuffed Spidey and took him away.

SEPTEMBER 16

A local blog, *Ybor City Stogie*, featured a video of my workout routine, which consisted of me hitting a punching bag: "Tim Fasano may look like an old man, but we're now certain that if anyone tries to mess with him, he's taken down hard. In this video, Fasano shows us his cardio routine. 'This is awesome cardio as I get in shape with weights and running to smash my haters in the mouth,' says Fasano."

SEPTEMBER 17

I picked a guy up at the airport, and he was going to the Tradewinds Hotel in St. Pete Beach. En route, he decided to do this conference call with his team about the big deal they were closing. I didn't mind, but it caused a problem when we arrived.

He tried to use a credit card to pay, but my system was down. It was stuck on processing. Since he was on a call, he didn't want to speak to the back office to clear up the matter. He kept talking on the phone about the big deal he was doing.

Well, I was doing a big deal for $73, and I wanted my damn money. He finally paid me in cash and acted pissed as if the tech error was my fault.

When I got back to my hotel room, I switched on the TV news and saw that just before 7:30 A.M. a store owner in the Cabaret Center strip mall drove into the rear parking lot and spotted an Allied Cab with a body inside. The police said the driver was shot between 1 and 2 A.M. Friends described him as a mild-mannered gentleman who liked working the night shift. A fellow cabbie who was interviewed said he heard about the killing while listening to the radio and drove to the parking lot. He knew a driver named Jack and hoped it wasn't him. It was.

SEPTEMBER 18

I was off to an address in the nice part of Southside

near Bayshore. I arrived at a lovely home, and a lady came out and asked if I could open the trunk. She needed some help. It turned out she was a caregiver for an older woman with a walker and had a good amount of items to load in the trunk. I could tell by their body language they weren't getting along. There was some tension. The caregiver simply went into the house and left me to load their stuff and help the lady into the back seat.

I drove her to a rehabilitation center to visit her sister. I got her and her stuff out of the cab — then helped her up the ramp with her things. The staff seemed to know her, and we continued to her sister's room. I told her that the fare was $11.45 and asked her politely for payment. She looked in her purse but couldn't find any money. "Don't worry, honey. My sister will pay you." She didn't tell me that it was her older sister, who was in a catatonic state.

When we got to the sister's room, she was staring out into space, eyes fixed, mouth agape. Was she even aware of our presence? I put the lady's stuff down and walked out of the room. Things didn't seem to be going very well today. It was about to get a little worse.

I walked out the door, and parked next to my taxi was an unmarked police cruiser — another cabbie cop. He wanted to know why I left my cab abandoned in a fire zone. I tried to explain to him that I was helping an elderly lady with her stuff. This seemed to calm him down, but just when I thought I was going to get away scot-free, he asked me why I wasn't wearing a shirt with a collar. This wasn't good.

These cabbie cops will write you a $30 ticket for no collar, and he didn't hesitate to do that. There was no way to talk him out of it. I told him that I was behind on the laundry, that I could've worn a dirty shirt but preferred to wear a clean one. He couldn't give a shit. He wrote the ticket, and I now have two weeks to pay it or be suspended. That taxi drivers are struggling out here means nothing to pricks like him. I threw the ticket on the dash and got ready for another call.

SEPTEMBER 19

After being diagnosed with deadly high blood pressure and chronic heart disease, I decided to do something about it. I tried walking, but with the Florida heat index of 105, all I do is cramp up. Swimming is low-impact exercise and invigorating, unlike jogging and other means of torture. Plus, you get some sun. I'm also lifting weights and trying to eat better. My goal is to compete in the Senior Nationals. I have a long way to go.

SEPTEMBER 20

I did some Bigfoot hunting today. I went into the Dead River area of Hillsborough County because it was a logging camp over eighty years ago. There've been numerous Bigfoot sightings in logging areas.

This place was desolate and spooky. I heard what I thought was Bigfoot tree-knocking although it may have been the sound of gunfire from poachers. (Hunting is illegal this time of year in Florida.)

This area is so remote and forbidden I don't think anyone else was out there but me. The reality of getting past the snakes, swamp, alligators, mud, sinkholes, and filth wouldn't be worth a poacher's time. Nonetheless, I posted a video that has a clear audio of what I think is Sasquatch tree-knocking, but I'm open to the idea it may be something else.

SEPTEMBER 21

The night air has an alluring quality. Over the years, I've seen people become intoxicated by it. Everything changes at night. Perceptions change after the midnight hour. The flow of traffic no longer dominates the urban sprawl.

As a night driver in the city, I've developed relationships with my surroundings. For example, the delivery man unloading milk behind the supermarket will become my friend even if we've never spoken, especially since this is where I often nap while waiting for a fare.

All was well tonight until the guy in the street sweeper woke me up with a sound louder than a jet engine. What gets me is that the parking lot never looks any cleaner after he's done.

SEPTEMBER 22

My friend Edgar — the guy I picked up in a bar in South Tampa last March, the guy who bought me tickets to the Rays games — passed away after a long bout with cancer.

Edgar turned out to be the type of friend everyone wants to have: the guy you hang out with on Saturday and crash on his couch and visit when you're bored. He was the friend who'd call if he hadn't heard from you in a few days.

His wife, Debbie, took care of him in the final weeks. He'll be missed by many.

SEPTEMBER 23

When I moved to Tampa from Sarasota in the late '80s, I settled into Hyde Park. The neighborhood had gone through transformations over the previous decades and was, at that time, in disrepair. What was once a quaint little place close to downtown and lined with pricey homes was now a thickly populated slum area.

I moved there because of the cheap rent in many of the subdivided houses and downscale apartments. Now rich yuppies live there. It's not so bad; it's just that they have no understanding of the history of the place, just like the real estate developers from Rhode Island who're buying up all the available properties.

SEPTEMBER 24

I got a 4 A.M. call to a home in South Tampa off Westshore — one of those beautiful mansions near the water. It was dark, and I had to use my spotlight to find the address. After shining the light at several houses, one house flicks the porch light — a sure sign of being at the right place. The door opened, and an older man was at the doorway. I was already out of the cab because I was expecting to load luggage for someone going to the airport. At this hour of the morning in that neighborhood, they weren't going to work at some fast food joint.

Out walks a young woman in a miniskirt, wearing six-inch heels. She told me she was going to Harbor Island as she slid into the cab. We drove for a few minutes in silence before she said, "I'm not a call girl," and began telling me about this guy she loved. He was a doctor and a drug addict. I guess everyone has their problems. At this point, her cell phone rang, and after talking to two different people, she said she had a new destination.

We now were on our way to a condo in downtown Tampa. After getting by the security guard, we pulled into a gated community. She called someone who said they were on their way down. Within a few minutes, a middle-aged couple appeared. They opened the back door and let her out. The man wanted to know how much the cab fare was and paid me, plus a generous tip. His wife kept eyeing the woman, repeating, "You're hot. You're hot. My God, you're hot."

Good first impressions are essential, no matter what line of work you're in. How do you spell *ménage à trois*?

SEPTEMBER 25

I picked up a young man at a local hotel who was headed to the Florida Championship Wrestling headquarters. His muscles and long blonde hair pegged him as a performer. He told me he was in town for an audition.

Tampa has always been a wrestling town, going back to Dusty Rhodes and "Superstar" Billy Graham. The armory packed them in every week for decades.

When we arrived at the facilities, there was a long line of good-looking, fit young people who were part of a casting call.

Tampa is a training ground for World Wrestling Entertainment, Inc. and other big-league federations.

Anyway, they get my vote. Good luck to all.

SEPTEMBER 26

After the bars closed this morning, I got a call at the Radiant store at Howard and Kennedy. The manager came out and said a guy was drunk and needed to go home to Pasco County. I asked the manager if the guy had any money. He said his father did and would pay me when I got there.

This guy came out with a girl, and the girl said she had just met the young drunk but had spoken to his father. Everything was cool. Well, everything wasn't cool. I told her I couldn't drive up to SR 52 on speculation. She said to talk to his father and handed me the phone. The drunk guy's name was Cory, and she said his father's name was Cody.

A youthful-voiced "Cody" said he was good for it. He also knew that it was twenty-six miles from downtown Tampa to his house. Good. I let him know that 26 x $2.25 a mile plus two bucks on the drop would be about $60. I heard crickets on the other end.

The chick now pulled the phone out of my hand and said, "Forget it. I'll take him. You seem to have a suspicious mind."

I've heard that a lot lately. I told her I didn't need her business and left both of them there.

My next fare was this geek-squad-looking guy going to the airport. He asked me how long I'd been driving a cab. Predictably people will then ask you if you do anything else with your time. It seems they want to believe we're just doing this until something better comes along. Then they'll always say they drove a cab in college or when they were starting out in life. Nobody wants to admit they drove a hack because they needed the money. What's wrong with that?

"I used to drive a cab once." He said it just like I knew he would. "Do you do anything else?"

"Yes." I told him I was learning digital photography and that most of my spare time was devoted to it. That I'd started a few websites, and my goal was to monetize them. He believed twenty to thirty thousand hits a day was the objective. I'm not getting traffic anywhere near that.

SEPTEMBER 27

For the absolute best burger in Tampa Bay, go to Five Guys located at the corner of Kennedy and Clark just west of Dale Mabry. I've never eaten a better burger. You won't go away hungry.

I picked up the owner/manager at his residence and took him to Five Guys so that he could open at 11 A.M. I'm not a fan of these overpriced, poor-service joints. I did notice that when we pulled into the parking lot, there was a line. What? A line at a burger joint? The manager paid me the fair and went in. It was 10:58 A.M. and they were about to open. So I parked and went in.

The first thing I noticed was the large space with lots of room and the high energy of the people who worked there. This was different than the sterile atmosphere at most fast food places. I got served by a courteous worker and ordered my burger all the way with fries. What I got amazed me.

The burger was too big to put in my mouth. I had to kind of work at it from the side. It was hot and delicious. There were also about 3 lbs. of fries to go with the order. I thought it was a mistake. I asked the manager, and he said all orders came with that many fries. I'm a big eater, and I couldn't finish it.

SEPTEMBER 28

I wanted to throw this guy and his girlfriend out of my cab. I've done it before with many asshole passengers. For some reason, people think we have to take their abuse. They couldn't be more wrong. I've put people out in parking lots, alleys, junkyards, wherever I can. Sometimes I don't go ten feet before I put people out. I learned my lesson the hard way when I was new to the business. I'd picked up a drunk at a bar and asked him where he was going. He said, "Just drive, asshole."

Many people will ask you if you're going to run the meter when they're out of the cab. This is what I do for a living, and of course I'm going to run the meter. I need to get paid. The Tampa Transportation Authority allows us to charge waiting time. The truth is most cab drivers don't like waiting, especially when we're busy. The meter runs at 45 cents every minute and a half — not much. Taxi drivers like to hustle and go. However, we're there to serve the public and will wait if that's what the fare wants.

There've been several meter rate hikes since I started in the business, none of them any good for drivers. The reason is that the taxi companies also raise the lease rates they charge their drivers. The TTA was created to benefit the taxi companies while soaking the drivers and making them shoulder the load. The current rates are too damn high in this economy, with gas approaching four bucks a gallon.

Some drivers work a twelve-hour shift for $75. When you factor in that drivers pay for their gas, this isn't such a good deal. A 24-hour driver pays $102 a day but keeps the cab and takes it home. Weekly drivers pay $500 a week plus gas. Most drivers (like me) are indigent and have no cars of their own, so this arrangement appeals to them. This is why we need to keep the cab moving. It used to take the first part of my day to cover expenses, but now it can take all day just to break even.

SEPTEMBER 30

My mom and dad were married on this day in 1944. I pray they're in paradise and I may one day see them again. I have a black-and-white photo of their wedding party, which includs my grandparents and other relatives, several of whom were born in the 1890s. Amazing.

OCTOBER

OCTOBER 1

A touch of autumn is in the air, and I love it. After six months of extreme heat, this is a welcome relief. Many people have commented on how wonderful this change of weather feels to them. I can go to work in the morning without my shirt sticking to my back and read the morning newspaper with the windows down and enjoy the fresh air. It's about time. This type of weather calms people down. They aren't so snappy.

OCTOBER 2

When I was young and beautiful, I was mixed up and had essentially no relationship with my parents. I felt I was not understood or respected. As a result, I began forming relationships outside of the house that didn't involve teenage girls or jock-type guys. I developed friendships with older men, most of them gay. Why? They were smart, witty, worldly, intuitive, clever, funny, opinionated, experienced, and made me feel important. My ideas were not immediately shot down the way my parents always did. They actually listened.

OCTOBER 3

I was crossing the Brorein Street Bridge into Hyde Park this morning when a lady began blasting her horn, tailgating me, and flashing her high beams. I kept going. She sped around me and motioned for me to pull over. So I did.

"How do you get to Brorein Street?" she asked.

"You're on it."

"I'm looking for the Marriott Waterside."

"Good luck," I said and sped off.

This is a common situation for taxi drivers. We're constantly hounded by people looking for directions.

I was parked, trying to eat my sandwich, when an older man pulled up and wanted to know how to get to the Social Security office. He was ten miles away, and I could tell by the look on his face he'd never find it. While I was talking to him, two more cars lined up behind him. I took off and found some shade in a nearby park to eat my lunch in peace.

On the way home, I stopped for a six-pack, and when I was getting back in my cab, a car stopped, and some guy came running up to me and wanted to know where US 301 was. He said he was looking for the LOTTO office. "What did you win?" I asked. He said a piece of the Fantasy Five. $700 bucks.

I should make a little sign: DIRECTIONS $5.

OCTOBER 4

I was dreaming today about an Arizona vacation

and remembered the last time I was there. It was night, and I could see the mountains behind downtown Phoenix. I watched the lights up above the mountain range, and I thought they must be the lights on top of some radio towers although they looked a little high up to be radio lights. I didn't think of it again until today. I did some online research and discovered something curious — that lights over Phoenix are a common sight. People have videotaped them and posted footage on UFO websites. Who knows what's going on in the desert?

OCTOBER 5

I had to renew my hack license today. The cab commission told me I was one of the longest-term drivers they have on file. I'm proud of that. Taxi driving is the only thing I've stuck with in my life. It shows I can commit, and I have integrity. The fee was $75. It was $10 my first year driving.

Today my right rear tire was leaking air, and I took it to Joe. He found a small screw stuck in the tire. Joe knew to do a soft plug because the standard size would only make the hole bigger.

OCTOBER 6

On STAND 23 there's this little kitty that's been hanging around. He's solid gray, and I think he's homeless. We named him "Smokey." I know that's not an original name for a gray cat, but that's what we named him.

We put food out for him although he looks well fed. There's a Burger King and a Chili's nearby, and I know he smells the meat cooking.

OCTOBER 7

I think I may have witnessed a crime. On my way home today, I stopped at a convenience store, and there was a lady in front of me with a three-year-old. She walked and talked ghetto. She was buying Swisher Sweets. Her little boy was acting curiously, touching items on display, which is typical for a little kid. His mother was visibly agitated. After she paid for the blunts, she grabbed his arm and yanked him, yanked him hard, and yelled, "Come on! We gotta go!" The little guy hit the floor. He didn't trip but was thrown to the floor.

When they left, the clerk and I both agreed we'd just witnessed child abuse. Should I have called the police? I had my cell phone with me. They were leaving the property, and by the time the cops got there, they would've been gone. Could I have done something? I don't know. I wish I had a do-over. There were two witnesses to the crime. She might've gone to jail and her kid to social services.

OCTOBER 8

I travel up and down Kennedy Boulevard every day and see things the average person driving an SUV and talking on a cell phone never will.

Kennedy Boulevard has come a long way from the seedy bars and blood plasma donation centers that littered this stretch of road twenty years ago.

Abraham Lincoln once observed, "Nearly all men can stand adversity, but if you want to test a man's character, give him power." I suspect our 16th president had Tampa's mayor in mind. Mayor Frank Fazzio spearheaded an aggressive policy of driving "unwanted" people to where? Other parts of Tampa? Or to the areas where the wealthiest of campaign contributors don't live. This head-in-the sand tactic seems to have worked on the surface, but I don't see any results. There are as many homeless today, if not more, than when he took office.

I see the homeless everywhere — like the guy who's always dumpster diving behind the check cashing place on Habana Avenue, looking for his next meal or anything of value. I don't know the guy, but I did talk to him briefly. He has a heart and soul and wants to live. I wish I had more time to listen to his personal story of heartache and disappointment, whatever it was that led to his downward spiral into this dumpster.

The dumpster sits behind one of the most corrupt businesses in Tampa. They cash checks for indigents and people with no bank accounts and rip them off more than the banks do with their fees. My twin brother, Tom, once handed me a book called *The Poor Pay More* by David Caplovitz, and it was an eyeopener about the "poverty penalty," how the poor end up paying more for almost everything: housing, clothing, transportation, food, etc.

I doubt if the Salvation Army would be of any help. They charge the homeless to live there. The problem is these folks have no money. How are they going to pay? I take people down there all the time, and I think the only reason they go is for the free dinner, which they've cut back on. They don't even serve lunch anymore.

OCTOBER 9

We were busy today. A convention was downtown, but I was unaware of it. I knew something was up when I was leaving downtown and got a call offer in the Westshore area. A call offer isn't a bid; it means it's a direct offer because nobody else can respond, which is rare. I got the call at 7:37 A.M. Despite the heavy morning traffic, I still made good time, getting there in twenty minutes.

The manager told me the fare was gone because I took too long. They got a ride with a co-worker. Great. I drove for nothing.

OCTOBER 10

People always want to know what's the craziest ride

I've had. The truth is, they're all crazy. Most trips, especially at night, turn into something a little weird. This is obvious after 4 A.M. Tammy used to say that's when "the creepy crawlies come out." What's crazy is that the creepy crawlies are the ones who want to know what your strangest ride was.

For example, I picked up a gay guy who wanted to go to the Cove Apartments. He had a quiet voice, but for some reason, he gave me the creeps.

"Any weird rides lately?"

"Yes, too many to count."

Like this ride, I was thinking.

He wanted to stop at an ATM about one mile from his home. After half a dozen tries to withdraw money, he gave up. He did have enough for the fare so far and said he'd walk the rest of the way home. I put him in the STRANGE category.

Nearby, I picked up these four college kids who wanted to go to the 2001 Odyssey strip club. They were stoned and wearing only boxer shorts and swim trunks. One of them had a big bag of potato chips, and all four of them were digging in and spilling chips all over the seat and floor.

They asked me what my name was, and I said, "Tim."

"Tim, what's the weirdest ride you ever had?"

I told them about the two hot chicks who were making out in the back seat. They started screaming and giving one another high fives.

When we got to the strip club, they got out, and one of them began dancing in the parking lot in his boxer shorts until one of his buddies reached out and yanked his shorts down to his knees. His buddies were jumping up and down like monkeys.

One guy got back in the cab and said he wanted to go to Brandon but had only $22. I told him it would cost more, but he didn't have his wallet because some chick had taken his clothes, and all he had on was his swim trunks. He said he had money at home and would pay me then. I took him, even though I knew he was going to burn me. When we got there, he went in and, of course, didn't come out. As I was starting to leave, he came out and paid me sixty bucks! In cash. Miracles never cease.

When I made it back to town, I got a call at the Holiday Inn. As I arrived, I saw the shuttle van (never a good sign). I got out of the cab, and the four people inside sat staring at me like zombies. Inside, the manager said Elvis already left the building. I said, "How did he leave?" the manager said, "Tampa Bay Taxi got him." I swear that company must be scanning our frequency. The feeling of being robbed was overwhelming.

OCTOBER 11

It's getting strange in a sort of good way. Unlike last year when the US Economy fell off the edge of the Earth, we're now having some good days thrown into the mix. The back office and the dispatchers say the call count is beginning to tick up. That's good news. So why are more and more people losing their jobs and foreclosing on their homes? I have no idea.

Unemployment may be a "lagging indicator" of where the economy is headed, but tell that to the people who can't pay their bills.

OCTOBER 12

A Seminole Heights man says he's talked to a neighbor about piles of trash and a house in disrepair. He says he's called the police and code enforcement. The man said none of that worked, so now he's turned to the Internet to document his dilemma.

He's posted photos of burnt piles of wood and the remains of a mattress in the backyard. His neighbor makes a lot of noise, and his girlfriend lets her kids camp out in the yard, which annoys the shit out of this guy. I can see why.

I went by the place and took a photo of this dilapidated eyesore. I saw swing sets and slides and monkey bars in the yard, and random junk I couldn't identify.

I've had problems with neighbors from time to time, and often, the only recourse is to move. They'll never change. The only thing I can control is myself. Getting out of there is something this guy might want to consider.

OCTOBER 13

The third week of October in Florida is a time that is special to residents. That is when the first cold front will make its way into the Sunshine State and bring us some real fall weather. I've waited a long time for this.

I went to a watershed north of Tampa, an area where Sasquatch prints have been discovered. My theory is that this is a prime area for exploration. I've been waiting months for the rainy season to end and cooler weather to settle in.

I felt the time was now to hike into the area to find prints. The place was thick with mud from months of endless rain, and waiting a week or so might not yield anything. I'm glad I went when I did because I found what I believe to be two different-sized footprints, which would mean an adult was walking with a young one, and they were walking side by side. I posted the video to YouTube.

OCTOBER 14

They're razing the dorm where I lived when I was a student at the University of South Florida. This was an active dorm back in the '80s. The rooms were small and close together. I don't think anyone ever slept in the place.

The wrecking ball reminded me of how old I am, the passage of time, and all that's inevitable.

OCTOBER 15

As I waited for my fare, I realized I was getting tired of most cab drivers. I've concluded that taxi drivers easily fall into two categories. There's the guy who always brags about the lucrative trips he's getting. This guy can't lose. The cab gods are on his side. Every day is an endless series of long fares and multiple trips that stack up as deep as the bullshit he's always slinging. Then there are the gloom-and-doom drivers. These guys are always getting screwed and having a bad day. They can't catch a break. Everyone is against them, the dispatchers, the phone operators, other drivers. Their paranoia is real, and they have proof to back it up. You almost wonder why they continue doing this for a living. I'd have lost hope.

Cab drivers have a lot of time to think and reflect on life. Perhaps that's at the root of their problem. What we do isn't healthy. The longer we're exposed to it, the more it warps our minds.

I've had many opportunities to wait for a fare and contemplate what's happening in my life. Maybe John Calvin was right. There are some people born to suffer.

I was thinking this while waiting at an apartment complex before two ladies came out and wanted to go to Sand Key Park in Clearwater. They were participating in the three-day walk to raise money for breast cancer. Now that's a worthy cause.

Traffic was jammed at five o'clock in the morning going in there. Three thousand ladies were going to walk a total of sixty miles each for the cause. I loved how hopeful these young women were.

After I dropped them off and was coming over the Causeway, I saw what had to be the most beautiful sunrise I've ever seen. Florida's climate after the first frost of the fall season produces colorful skys. This morning was extraordinary. Lately I've snapped some of the best shots of Florida sunrises I've ever taken. There's a reason to have hope after all.

OCTOBER 16

In the 1920s, the Tampa Hotel was the tallest building in Florida. It was *the* place to stay when visiting Tampa. Like many places, it had its moment, then fell on hard times.

When I moved to Tampa in the early '80s, it was still open. It had a bar on the ground floor with a pool table. My old boss from *The Tampa Tribune* and I would go in and have a beer after work. You could tell by the ornate architecture and artwork that it was once spectacular.

By the '70s, it'd become a vagrant hotel with weekly rentals to skid row types and prostitutes. It soon closed and has lain fallow ever since. There must be a reason. With the condo explosion, I thought this building would've been renovated by now, but for some reason it hasn't been.

OCTOBER 17

What's happening is way beyond just having "a bad day." Most drivers are getting somewhere between two to five calls a day. That's it.

"Don't worry, it'll be better tomorrow," a customer told me, but I am worried. Each day is exactly the same. For example, this morning I came out at 5 A.M. and didn't get a call until 9 A.M. This is the new normal.

The new dispatch system is inherently unfair. If you're not close to a call, it won't give you one, nor will it ever send you a bid. Without bids, I can't make any money. Syd Glaston said I need to park my cab where the calls are going to come out. How do I do that? The calls could come from anywhere. I'm not a psychic, so I'm screwed.

Talking to Syd and Eddie Munster (the computer guy) proved useless. They don't understand the algorithms that run the dispatch system. Syd said one day he'll call the main office and get an explanation. Great! That'll do me a lot of good while *I STARVE!*

One of the reasons I haven't left Allied Cab to go to Bay Cab is that I serve Lighthouse for the Blind & Low Vision. I enjoy working for them and don't want to give it up.

Working for another company, however, remains a viable option for me. I'm ready to work, and I need to work. With my years of experience, I would be an asset to any company that wants a seasoned driver, not just someone who can fog a mirror.

OCTOBER 18

A cabbie in New York City found a bag of diamonds on the back seat and went out of his way to return them. I know firsthand that returning items is a dicey situation for a cabbie. Over the years, people have left everything you can think of in my cab: cell phones, camcorders, glasses, cell phones, wallets, cell phones, car seats, purses, bags, laptops, cell phones, money, and even a TV. In most instances, I'd've been better off not trying to return them.

The reason is that people are never grateful I've taken the time to decline a call and go to their house to give them the item *they* left behind. A tip is rare. In fact, they often think I haven't returned everything. Years ago, when Pirate was dispatching on the weekends, I dropped some people off at the Cruise terminal, and the guy contacted me through the dispatch radio to see if he left behind a camcorder. I pulled off the road and looked. Sure enough, there was a camcorder case on the back seat. I immediately took off for the port to return it.

When I handed the man the case, he opened it and said, "Where's my camcorder?" He said the case was empty and I must've stolen it. I told him to suck my ass and took off.

The next week the back office told me they received a letter from him, and he wanted me to pay for the camcorder. I refused. They must've believed me because I never heard about it again.

OCTOBER 19

The tropical system that's hanging around Florida should soon push northward. Good weather should follow, and that'll mean money for taxi drivers in Tampa. Plus, things should be picking up this Saturday night with the Guavaween festival and parade (an annual Latin-flavored Halloween celebration in Ybor City). This used to be a real moneymaker for us, but in recent years its popularity has slipped. Troublemakers have ruined it for the families that used to attend.

OCTOBER 20

As the sun sets on the West Coast of Florida, something happens to people. Night-shift taxi drivers head out to make money in what's one of the truly nocturnal cities in America. Florida is the tourist capital of the world, and it isn't just about Mickey Mouse. Travelers come for many of Florida's vices, including prostitution, strip clubs, and dog and horse track gambling. They're drawn to Tampa because of its reputation. When they go out at night for fun, they drink, and they move club-to-club. That's when the cab business benefits. We're the designated drivers.

One benefit of working nights is it's cooler outside. It can be sweltering during the days, and if you're sitting around waiting for a fare, you'll have to run the air-conditioning, and that'll cost you money. Even the fares are different at night. During the day, people are going to work, the airport, their place of business. At night, all that changes. People are now out because they want to be out. They're in a better mood.

The streets aren't so jammed at night unless there's a major sporting event. We have pro teams in every sport, and in recent years, they've had the kind of success that brings fans out to the stadiums. Winning sports teams put money in cabbies' pockets.

Eventually, a driver will enter what my cab-driving friend

Roger calls "The Tumbleweed Hours," that two-hour span before the last call for alcohol. I almost wonder if the phones are down, it's so dead. Most clubs have unofficial cabstands in front. They're unofficial because the Transportation Commission doesn't prohibit them. Bar closing is like a jailbreak. It isn't spread out over several hours so that a driver can make consistent money. At 2 A.M. bar patrons pile out all at once, just like at the county jail when they release prisoners at the same time.

When things do settle down, I'm left with a sense of peace. I sit along the road with the windows down and breathe the tropical night air. It's at this moment when I'll break out a notebook and start jotting down ideas. I do my best thinking this time of the morning.

During the day, I'm dodging cars whose drivers are probably texting; I'm at a green light and honking at cars in front of me because they're not moving; I'm on the alert for drivers trying to beat the light. At night, that all changes.

There's a convenience store I park at late at night. A friend of mine, Noland, works the graveyard shift there, and I always look forward to seeing him. I met Noland years ago when I started driving a cab, and he's one of the smartest people I've ever known. He's a writer waiting for his break. Ask him anything, and he'll speak like an authority on it. I'll sit in a parking spot, waiting for Noland to take a break, and notice how many people just walk up out of the shadows, go in the store, then emerge and slip back into the night.

Noland came out for a smoke one night, and I asked him about this phenomenon. He said it happens all the time. They're drawn to the lights as if looking for some ray of comfort or truth. I thought about this for a moment and wondered what was noble and valiant about man's quest for his own humanity in the parking lot of a 7-Eleven. While I was thinking this, a drunk got out of his car and told us to fuck off. I blame it on the night air.

OCTOBER 21

For the last couple of days, the airport has been moving in the mornings. This is the time of year when things begin to pick up. The airport is crucial for making money, allowing me to cover most of my lease. There are cruise ships arriving at the port and conventions in town.

Today I also took a fare to Clearwater Beach, something I haven't done in a while. The best part was I didn't wait for hours to get a short fare, and the weather was beautiful. I hope it keeps up.

OCTOBER 22

One thing about cab driving is that your co-workers end up becoming your best friends. Unfortunately, most cab drivers spend so much time in their cabs there's little chance for any kind of social life.

OCTOBER 23

I had seven passengers in a row this morning who whipped out twenty-dollar bills to pay the fare. Many of the trips were short — like four or five bucks.

I don't start my day with hundreds of dollars in small bills. This morning I gave one of the passengers a freebie because I couldn't break his twenty-dollar bill. Yesterday, a guy in a hoodie handed me a hundred dollar bill for a $15 ride and thought I'd somehow produce the dead presidents.

I know most people think cab drivers will make change, but we're not the 7-Eleven, where a clerk can press a button and have a little canister come up with a resupply of new bills. I try my best, dropping by fast food and coffee joints to break down large bills, but I can't do that after every ride.

Cabbies don't carry lots of money because we don't want the word getting out that our pockets are stuffed with cash.

OCTOBER 24

Kate is dead. Two days ago her brother called me from North Carolina and asked me to do a welfare check on her at her mother's condominium, where she'd been staying since before New Year's. He hadn't been able to reach her by phone. So I drove down to Hudson, and when she failed to answer the door, I left a note.

This morning the note was still there. The curtain and blinds hadn't been moved, and the light in the hallway was still on. I was very alarmed. I found the maintenance man, and he had a master key for the door. It would work only for the door handle and not the deadlock bolt. I knew she was in trouble and kicked in the patio door. From the sliding glass door, through a crack in the curtain, we could see her body on the living room floor.

Why did I not do this Monday. If she was already dead, would that have made a difference? I called 911. It looked like she'd fallen and hit her head on the end table near the sofa. The detectives later concluded as much. At one time in her life, she was an aspiring dancer and actress, and she liked to dance after a few drinks.

I called her brother and relayed the horrible news. He was shocked but did say she'd been talking about suicide lately. That's why he was so concerned when he hadn't heard from her.

Her life was not always happy. She grew up in Tampa and went to King High School. She was extremely bright with a high IQ. She went on to Colombia in New York, where her mother was a music professor, but dropped out of school as the conditions of her mental illness took over her life.

This insidious disease kept us apart and ultimately took her life. One outcome of bipolar disorder is that their victims don't live very long. The chemical maelstrom whirling in their brains puts a strain on their internal organs. For the past few months, she kept telling me she was dying, usually telling me this over the phone when she was drunk. I thought it was the alcohol talking. Individuals with bipolar disorder often have some form of alcohol dependency.

She dabbled in modeling, for she was very pretty. She never married. Most men were intimidated by her. I was able to maintain a short relationship with her that ended five years ago, and we managed to remain friends afterwards. She left for a couple of years and recently moved into her mother's condo in Hudson. I visited her occasionally but knew something was not right. She asked me once, "What would you do if you knew you were dying?"

OCTOBER 25

I have no idea what the final arrangements are. Kate's brother is suddenly not answering his phone. I assume he's on his way down to Tampa. I do need some kind of closure. That's why I got the roses. I went up to Kate's condo today and put my hand on the door and could feel her energy. All of her personal items were inside, all of her nice clothes and pretty things. I told her how much I loved her and that I was glad she was not suffering anymore. Despite how problematic our friendship was, I will truly miss her.

OCTOBER 26

When I first started driving a cab in 1995, I used to roll through Hyde Park Village. Sometimes while crossing Rome Avenue, I'd see this attractive woman wearing a white smock crossing the street. I later found out she was one of the cosmetic salesgirls at Jacobson's Department Store. Her name was Kate. I used to stop for coffee at Joffrey's Coffee and Tea Company, and she would be in line and was pleasant and easy to talk to.

Jacobson's subsequently closed, and I lost touch with the cosmetic girl. Then one day on Christmas Eve 1999, I saw a beautiful woman standing at the bus stop at Britton Plaza. It was the Jacobson's girl.

I pulled up and asked her if she needed a cab.

She said, "I think I know you."

We drove around while she told me what was going on in her life. It was the holiday season, and I was lonely so I asked her if she wanted to go to dinner. We went to the Steak and Ale in Temple Terrace. We had a great time, and I invited her over to my apartment. She accepted.

We chatted, watched TV, and she told me she was a model and actress. She worked in local community theater and knew Larry, my fellow cabbie and friend, who was also active in local theater. I found her personable, witty, smart, and talented.

OCTOBER 27

My impression of Kate was that she had a kind soul and was committed to noble causes. However, as time went by I began to realize she had a much darker side.

I've pored over my journals and have found entries in which I wrote "delusional" and "psychosis." I made notes that she didn't sleep. She stayed up all night the short time she was with me. I later learned this was a common symptom of some types of mental illness. I told her I couldn't live with someone who was up all night. It wasn't possible for me to do that. We argued about this but resolved nothing.

Two weeks after she moved in with me, she disappeared, leaving behind most of her stuff. I called her brother and left a message. He didn't call back but Kate's mother did and said she'd been trying for years to get help for her daughter, but the state of Florida was useless when it came to mental health services. All they were told was she was on a waiting list with thousands of others trying to get a Medicaid waiver through the Florida Agency for Persons with Disabilities, which is millions of dollars underfunded, like every damn thing else in the Sunshine State.

OCTOBER 28

An article in *The Tampa Tribune* this morning was headlined: CABDRIVER FINDS FRIEND DEAD AFTER WEEK WITHOUT CONTACT: AUTOPSY PLANNED TO DETERMINE CAUSE. I was quoted as saying, "I think she was drinking some wine and doing some dance maneuvers and fell."

After work, I went to Allied Cab to sign the new contract. I was talking to Jean, and she said she saw me on BAY NEWS 9 the day Kate died. She seemed concerned about me and wanted to know what my relationship to Kate was and how I was holding up. I told her Kate was a close friend, and I thanked her for her concern.

At this moment, Marjorie came in and said, "Does it take you that long to sign a contract?"

Some people are just rude.

OCTOBER 29

Cab drivers often turn down fares, and it has nothing to do with racism or hate. Most of the time it involves our safety and concern about being paid.

I got a call at 4:30 A.M. to a new condo project in South Westshore. It's so new, it's not even on the map. Ibrahim told me the first cab that responded to this call had a problem with them and pulled off the call. The fare called back, and I got it. "Oh, Christ," that's what any cab driver would think. The first guy turned it down because at this hour the people were probably drunk and disorderly and gave him a hard time. That was not exactly what was going on.

When I got there a woman came out and got in the cab. She was drunk, and her boyfriend was still inside. He then came out, and she was arguing with him through the back-seat window. He had her cell phone and threw it about a hundred feet across the parking lot, where it shattered. She got out of the cab.

"You asshole!" she yelled.

She found what was left of her phone and went over to him and started swinging with balled-up fists.

She screamed the N-word at him and said, "My phone is my own damn business!"

Apparently he'd found other guys' phone numbers on her cell phone.

I took off. These types of situations are common on the weekend when people are drunk. It has nothing to do with race. I don't like that kind of shit and refuse to have anything to do with it.

Later, I was getting gas at the Shell at Kennedy and Howard, and this cracked-out looking guy comes up to the cab, and he's agitated and wants to know if I'm available. No, I told him. I've been doing this a long time, and I know he probably wants to go to some sketchy neighborhood and put me at potential risk. This is a law enforcement problem, not a transportation one. I wish the cops would clean up these areas so I could work and not fear for my life.

OCTOBER 30

Some of the leaves have turned colors and daytime lows are now in the low 70s. Big deal, right? For us Floridians, it's a welcome relief from the extreme heat and humidity we've had for the last seven months. This is always my favorite time of year. I can now get out on expeditions and do overnight camping without the bugs eating me alive.

OCTOBER 31

It happened again today. This time it was a bad one — a traffic accident at the intersection of Kennedy and Howard. I go through this stretch of road all the time, and when the light turns yellow, people speed up to beat it. Often vehicles continue to go through the intersection after it's red.

Today I was northbound in the left-hand turn lane on Howard, getting ready to turn westbound on Kennedy when I heard a horn blowing. Often people who want directions honk at me. I looked around but saw nobody waving at me. The horn continued to blast, sounding far away. I was beginning to get spooked, then the light turned green. Looking both ways, I began to drive slowly, but the woman in a minivan to my right gunned it. An eastbound van sped through the light and broadsided her.

Was it a guardian angel making that honking sound? I don't know. I only know that when traffic lights turn green, I'm usually off to the races. I wish that woman hadn't gunned it the way she did. She was hurt and bleeding, and her daughter was screaming and crying. I pulled over and called 911. The man driving the van climbed out, cell phone stuck to his ear, looking like someone had taken a pair of pliers to his testicles. Maybe he was calling 911 too, but I doubt it.

NOVEMBER

NOVEMBER 1

I was interviewed by the *St. Petersburg Times* for an upcoming article about the taxi business in Tampa.

The impetus of the article was the recent release of forty-seven new taxi permits for the city of Tampa and the purported purchase of the licenses by an outside company called Metro, which presents a threat to the established companies.

The reporter said she'd spoken to Sam Lebowitz, president of the the Tampa Public Transportation Commission. She also talked to Bay Cab and Allied Cab. What I told the reporter were the following points: 1) Free markets aren't feasible in the taxi industry; 2) Start-up companies don't serve the interest of the public; 3) Sam Lebowitz has a flawed understanding of the taxi business.

Free markets aren't applicable in the cab business. Unlike other trades or professions with qualifications, such as some type of training or education, cab driving has no restrictions. No matter how many permits there are, someone will fill them. Forty or four hundred — it doesn't matter as long as a prospective driver has a pulse. In addition, cab driving has no balancing point because being a cabbie is a way of life — a subculture. Unless you work hard with a goal to get out of it, you never will. Cab drivers will live out of a motel, a homeless shelter; sleep on the backseat of their cab if they have to. The one thing they'll not do is stop driving. There's no profession where this happens, and the owners of the cab companies know it. That's why they'll keep raising the lease — drivers will keeping paying it.

Start-up companies don't serve the public. The reason is that they only hire drivers who've been fired from other companies. That leaves them with mediocre cabbies. Since the start-ups are new, they have no street business, and their drivers only work the hotels and cruise ships and bars. The public isn't served.

Sam Lebowitz believes they're served, and that's the problem. Lebowitz was an Army officer in charge of transportation and logistics. That's great if you're moving supplies and tanks to the field, but not if your managing a city's cab industry. Since he's been commissioner, he's forced up leases because of meter rate hikes. Meter increases don't help drivers. Only the companies benefit. Lebowitz has also levied fines on drivers for a litany of petty infractions. I once got a $20 fine for having a rip in the kneecap of a pair of jeans.

NOVEMBER 2

We work weird hours. Often, we're looking for fresh

coffee at convenience stores in the middle of the night. What usually happens is the coffee they serve has been sitting for 6–7 hours. Coffee has a holding time of about twenty minutes.

The Starbucks on south Howard is now open 24/7. I went in this morning at 4 A.M., and fresh, really fresh coffee (dark roast) was being served. Fresh coffee is important to cab drivers and people who work in the middle of the night, like cops and paramedics.

NOVEMBER 3

Today was Election Day in the U.S.A. It's an off year, so there wasn't much going on in most states.

I remember voting in the Florida Primary last year; and as I was coming out of the polling place, a photographer from the *Washington Post*, Linda Davidson, snapped my picture as I waved to her. The photo was published on their website with the following caption: "Tim Fasano, 52, shows off his 'I Voted' sticker next to his Buccaneer patch at a voting precinct in north downtown Tampa, Florida. Fasano is Italian and has lived in Tampa the last fifteen years. Ybor City, nearby, is home to a lot of Hispanics, Italians and African Americans. Its history dates back to the day when cigar factories were steady work here."

NOVEMBER 4

Every time I go into Syd Glaston's office, there's a driver in there bitching about the tablets Allied installed. The problems are inaccurate GPS, no GPS, long response time, choking on data, phantom call offers, knocking drivers out of zones, locking up after every call, constant reboots, failure to check drivers into new zones, auto posts always down, losing proximity calls to drivers farther away, telling drivers they must wait sixty seconds to post because of some error.

Syd always says, "Someone's working on it."

NOVEMBER 5

It seems when strippers pay the fare, it's always in crumbled, grubby bills. I don't mind taking the money although I do know where that money has been. This chick I picked up tonight had a bunch of ones. She was nice, which isn't always the case with strippers. Many of them are arrogant and unpleasant.

NOVEMBER 6

Louis Tillman is accused of killing cab driver Linda Faison in a brutal attack last July. Police believe he stabbed her over 200 times and then ran her body over with her cab. Stabbing someone is a more personal way of killing than shooting them. Utilizing a knife requires close contact, and the fact that she was stabbed hundreds of times suggests a very strong level of hatred. This is an aspect of serial killing, where there's a perverse satisfaction derived from the murder.

What's almost impossible to believe about this case is that this guy at one time was serving ten years in prison for armed robbery and burglary. He's only twenty-two, and they let him out. We had this guy behind bars, and then he was released. Unbelievable.

NOVEMBER 7

He was just trying to survive like I am. I've been driving for fourteen years, and I've regularly picked Dave up over the years. He used to live on Wisconsin Avenue until he was evicted. I picked him up today at the Crosstown Inn, a sort of rundown motel at Dale Mabry and Gandy.

He needed to go to Metropolitan Ministries because that's where his mail is now delivered. I agreed to take him to pick up his Social Security check and then drive him to Amscot. It sounded simple. It got a little complicated.

He went inside the Mission, which was crowded with

people picking up boxes of food and waiting in line for what the sign on the door said: FOOD, MONEY, LIVING EXPENSES.

I noticed that the parking lot was full of new and late model cars. That pissed me off.

Many times in my life, I've had to sell a car or other things to get money to eat. These people aren't making a sacrifice. I don't own a car, and I don't beg.

The guy came out and said his check wasn't there, and we needed to go back to South Tampa to the post office. He was completely ignoring the $25 on the meter.

I was sensitive to his plight, but I can't run the meter up to fifty or sixty bucks on speculation that I might get paid. I was tempted to leave his sorry ass behind, but instead I drove him to the post office, where miraculously he found his check. After cashing it at Amscot, I charged him only the initial $25.

If we don't help those worse off, then who will help us in our time of need?

NOVEMBER 8

We're now on the new system where both Allied Cab and Bay Cab are on the same side of the airport. We're on the west quad, and we will be for the next three years because of construction. It's a significant project that'll result in a larger and more efficient airport. The airport is going to tear down the Marriott and convert it into a shopping mall. This project will allow more people to move quickly through the airport.

NOVEMBER 9

This morning I was sitting in the holding area at the airport, listening to the guys jibber-jabber on the radio. Their talk gets everybody all excited in the mornings. The thing about when you're down in line is you're not exactly in the catbird seat. You don't know where the fares are going. It could be a

$15 minimum; it could go out to St. Pete Beach. It could go anywhere. We're working on commission like salesclerks. It's like getting dealt cards in a blackjack game. You hope you can get that natural 21, but there's not much you can do. We do have fair and honest starters now that Fred was fired. They're going to load cabs precisely the way they're ordered. I'd rather have starters because without them drivers would cheat.

NOVEMBER 10

The taxi business is dead in the United States. This industry is going the way of payphones, Fotomats, and video stores. Did I mention Kodak film?

Like every cabbie I know, I'm a rolling anachronism. I can't make a living. I'll probably soon be evicted from my cheap motel. I can't pay the rent or any other bill. My life is a shambles, and I face an uncertain future. Is there anything more to say?

NOVEMBER 11

I hit the Florida Trail over the weekend. I went to a remote part near the Withlacoochee River south of the Ocala National Forest. It was very quiet, and I saw lots of wildlife. I did get pictures of something that might've been a black bear or a tree stump. It seemed to be sitting on a creek bank. I found a primitive camp site and lit a campfire. I got some great images and lots of video I'm still looking at.

The Florida trail is 1,100 miles long and stretches from south of Miami all the way up to the Panhandle of Florida near the Alabama border. It cuts through the rich ecosystem that is unique to Florida and into the most remote parts of the North American Continent. That is where a Large mammal could hide and live without ever being spotted. That's why I plan to explore the entire trail.

I'm working on a plan that'll put me on the Florida Trail

at the halfway point in the Green Swamp of Polk County and up into the Panhandle. It will take me about eight weeks to walk this trail and do all of the photography and squatching I need to do. Camping out at night, isolated miles from civilization, it'll be a golden opportunity I wouldn't want to pass up. I plan to start on February 15 of next year.

The Tampa Tribune reporter Mike Dewitt said it all when he walked the Florida Trail in 2007: "Florida's soul is on this trail."

NOVEMBER 12

Many long-term drivers know John. He used to work only days and only in the Gandy area of Tampa. He switched to the airport when the economy went south in 2008; he's stayed at the airport ever since. Like a lot of older drivers, he limits his activities.

I was in line with him this morning.

"Glad to see you, John. How're you doing? How's your leg." I could see his cane leaning against the front seat.

"All right. Good. I got cortisone shots the other day so they helped a little bit, but I can't take the time off. I can't afford it."

"I saw that one day you were turning the cab in and you were gonna go have your surgery, and then I heard you didn't have the surgery."

"No, no, I chickened out, I guess."

"How's business out here?"

"You know, every afternoon I've been getting a good ride, every fucking afternoon. St. Pete Beach."

"Yeah, I've been getting that too."

"Every afternoon, three–four o'clock."

"What few I get seem to be going somewhere."

John, despite his age and health problems, maintains a positive attitude in his own way. He always cheers me up.

NOVEMBER 13

I've been very sick lately. I'm on steroid treatment for inflammation in my head. That's been why I've been dizzy and sick. I had all the symptoms of a mini-stroke. The ER released me, and my primary hopes are that this treatment works.

NOVEMBER 14

As I was dropping a fare off on a country road, I saw a beautiful sunrise stretching to the horizon. To me, it symbolized life, the spiritual road we find ourselves on in this existence. Often, in times of despair, people think they're at the end of their rope. That's not a good metaphor.

We're more like on a road. There's nothing we can do about that. The road is laid out in front of us, and we must proceed. Decisions we make along the way will determine the direction we take. I've lived long enough to know fate can often intervene and have more control over us than we want to believe.

That's why people develop beliefs to control their fears — religious or spiritual, even secular in just knowing you're a good person and your life has meaning. Perhaps that's why people yearn to tell their story, to separate themselves from the hordes out there. There's an acronym in AA called HALT — hungry, angry, lonely, and tired. These are trigger points. Things that can and will push your buttons and, for a moment, cause you to lose direction. People do react in different ways.

The fear people have is that their story won't get told or they'll leave it to someone else to tell it. Don't let that happen. The reasons people blog are deeply personal. At least they are with me. There are no financial rewards. Nobody is making any money at it, but in lieu of money and fame, your story can still be told — a testament to you and what you were all about.

NOVEMBER 15

When I was in Ybor City this morning, I decided to take a look around. Tampa (like San Francisco) has a rich cable car history. There was a time when cigar shops and immigrant workers depended on this form of transportation.

There's a monument in Ybor to these workers and the city they helped build. Near Avenida Republica de Cuba there are two chairs by the train station. They're bronzed. The plaque says these are the chairs the cigar workers sat on all day as they hand rolled cigars. Ironically, the building in the background was a factory that's now protected by historical preservation law.

Life was tough back then. Now the cable cars are used by tourists. I've had plenty who told me to take them to Ybor so they can check it out. I always try to give them a quick history lesson so they can at least appreciate what they see.

NOVEMBER 16

I needed to buy a cheap pair of gym shoes today (I've started working out again), and I finally had the money to buy them. So I headed for the Walmart at Dale Mabry and Spruce. As I pulled in, the channel one dispatcher said there was a fare at the front of the store. Great! I could get my shoes some other time.

I saw what looked like a tent city. Apparently, there were people camped out, waiting since midnight Friday to buy the latest version of PlayStation. To be honest, there was nobody in that line who looked as if they had the $500 this thing costs.

I rolled by the front of the store, and this elderly lady with a worried look on her face waved to me. I pulled in, and she said, "I've called twice and been waiting thirty minutes.

I said *No problemo*. (You like my Spanish?)

I got out and began to load her bags into the trunk. As I was doing this, a man with a vest got out of a little car with flashing lights and started writing down my tag number. I asked him what the problem was and why he was recording my car info. He said I violated "1720-6b." The front of the store was a fire lane, just like any of the hundreds of other stores where we pick up. He said he was going to report me to the taxi commission and have my taxi license revoked.

I began unloading the lady's bags. He wanted to know what I was doing. I told him I was leaving and slammed the trunk.

He said, "Aren't you going to take her home?"

"Not if it's going to cost me my job."

I drove off.

In the rearview mirror, this Barney Fife wannabe was staring at me, mouth agape. She must've given him hell because she called back, and another cab was allowed to load.

NOVEMBER 17

An unregulated free taxi service was recently started in Tampa that was mostly a glorified golf cart. It was unsafe, uninsurable, and a public safety hazard. The Tampa Public Transportation Commission did the right thing in shutting it down.

To get a hack permit in Tampa, you must go through a background screening, including mugshots, fingerprinting, and an FBI database check. The public is protected because they're not being picked up by dangerous criminals.

The commission also has requirements on the mechanical condition and cleanliness of taxis and dress code requirements for drivers.

NOVEMBER 18

A lot is going on in Tampa right now. The weather is beautiful, and people can take advantage of outdoor activities they couldn't during the heat. Best of all, our business is way up.

Unfortunately, I've been in bed since Wednesday night

with the flu. It hit me like a ton of bricks. When it did, I could hardly pick myself up to get in bed, and there I lay until Friday morning.

The phone rang several times from friends who wanted to know what happened to me. I could barely talk, but I told them all the same thing. "Did you hear the Pope got bird flu? He got it from the Cardinals." Is that laughter I hear?

For the first twelve hours, you think you're going to die. Then you're afraid you won't.

I'm feeling better and should soon be on the road again.

NOVEMBER 19

The Ocala National Forest is a 430,000 acre preserve. It was the first national forest east of the Mississippi River and is the southernmost. It is also one of the best areas in the country for Bigfoot sightings. That's why this area has been on my radar for months. I've just been waiting for the weather to cool down.

I spent a weekend there and got a lot of footage to upload to my YouTube station. I'm in the process of editing the videos. I got some great nature photos that made it worth the trip. Unfortunately, I did not have a Bigfoot sighting. Neither did I expect to spot one my first time coming up here.

I've scouted out many primitive camping areas and will be taking some overnights deep into the forest in the coming months. Some exciting things are in the works. I hope to have some positive evidence by early next year.

The Ocala National Forest is a beautiful and adventurous place. I can't believe it's taken me so long to get up here.

NOVEMBER 20

When a taxi driver comes to work early in the morning, he can tell if it was busy the night before by checking how many cabs are posted in zones.

Combine the cabs Allied had out with the number of Bay cabs, plus the cabs from smaller companies, and there were over 130 taxis out before sunrise this Tuesday. It's the slowest time of the week. Do we need that many cabs?

NOVEMBER 21

The last few years the taxi business in Tampa has been rough. I'm not going to lie. I have a good day now and then, but most days are crap. I'm hanging by a thread in all aspects of my life and may be facing homelessness. That's something I'm trying to avoid.

I owe the company over $1,000, and that's the benchmark at which they let drivers go.

It's a month before Christmas, and that'd be a shitty time to get thrown to the curb. We're only days away from the good time of the year, and my life depends on this. I'm too old to be walking down the street with just the clothes on my back, knowing that I could be making money.

NOVEMBER 22

Just when I was about to despair, today was insanely busy at the airport. The airlines must be doing a record business. They say travel is up from last year. I believe it.

I think the only reason people were taking our cabs today was that the parking lots were full. We could still use more business because this has been a slow month. I'm not going to have much of a holiday this year. As Larry always believed: happiness is on the way.

This morning I picked up a couple at Post Hyde Park Apartments on South Fremont and took them to the airport. They were on their way to Louisiana to enjoy some crayfish and turkey. When I picked up my next fare, she handed me a purse and said someone must've left it.

The purse had an entire life in it: credit cards, ID, and

cash. How would she get on the plane? I went back to the airport although Billy said to wait until they called us. She needed her purse and fast. I went to American Airlines and gave it to the front desk. They confirmed that a lady by that name was traveling with them, and they would make sure she got it. Good. Some other driver might've taken her cash and thrown the purse away.

NOVEMBER 23

The Tampa police were at Allied Cab this morning. We've had drivers get robbed in the parking lot, but last night someone was robbed out front — not a driver but a man walking by the shop. Why would anyone be out for a stroll at four in the morning? I know this area is going to get better, but not right now. I think the guy was out here to score drugs and ran inside our office after he was held up. The cops didn't seem too concerned about it.

NOVEMBER 24

For many years West Tampa has been down on its luck. What was once the premier place to live has for decades been a slum and industrial area. That's changing now.

I had to stop by our office, which is located on the corner of Cass and Rome. As I was walking out to my cab (I always park on the street), I could see how fast they're putting up the luxury condos across the street. What happened south of Kennedy Boulevard is now happening north of Kennedy.

I wonder where the poor people are going to live. Builders squeezed them out of Central Park, and now they're making inroads into West Kennedy.

This part of town is one of our most impoverished service areas. Cab drivers don't like responding to calls here because they're problematic. Locals don't go far, they don't have any money, they don't tip. Besides, I don't like watching young baby mamas beat their kids and yell and scream — none of it's good for my blood pressure.

NOVEMBER 25

I checked into ZONE 32 at 4:50 A.M. I was ready to work and had a good attitude. I had a good night's sleep and a fresh cup of coffee. I was ready to serve. Boy, was I wrong.

Minutes became hours, and I received no bids. Not one. By 8 A.M. I still had no calls. I was posted #1 in a very large zone with a diverse demographic. Again, no bids.

A driver pulled up next to me. He said he just came out and wanted to know if it was busy. I told him how slow it was and that he hadn't missed a damn thing. At that very instant we both got bids. He won the bid. The computer screwed me. The call was going to the airport too.

I wasn't amused. I'm in trouble with the company for owing them money. There just aren't enough calls to support a fleet 300 strong.

I'll have to see what comes first: losing my job or getting evicted from my hotel room. With my luck, it'll be both on the same day. I've opened a PayPal account and will soon have a link for donations. It's about the only thing I can do. It'll help me buy food.

NOVEMBER 26

Thanksgiving. I bought some sliced turkey at Publix and heated it up in the microwave. Gobble, gobble.

NOVEMBER 27

I dropped a stripper off at a club where she'd parked her Mercedes. There must be money in getting naked. Nude dancing is a major industry in Tampa, so maybe I should take a pole dancing class. Meanwhile, $25 for a $20 fare will keep me from taking my clothes off. Most would pay me to keep them on.

NOVEMBER 28

Thirty-nine days until this awful year is finally over. Quite a statement when we count toward nothing.

NOVEMBER 29

I picked up a guy at the Howard Johnson's on Dale Mabry, and he said he came in late last night; and the reason he was there was all the hotels had NO VACANCY signs. What? Then where are the customers? Is it like the Shriners convention, the hotels full and nobody using cabs? I did pick this guy up from Canada on North Westshore and after waiting five minutes for him to find an address on his laptop (in the old days he would've had a piece of paper with it written down), we finally find out he's going four blocks. He did give me ten bucks, however.

I worked nine hours today and only drove 62 miles. I should've driven 162 miles. It's November, the holidays are supposed to be around the corner. It can only get better, right?

NOVEMBER 30

I drive up and down Memorial Highway in Town and Country and I often see a wooden sign that says PAM CALLAHAN NATURE PRESERVE. Today I stopped by to see what it was all about.

You have to park on the side of the road and there's a gate that's locked, but you can easily go around it. This seemed to be a maintained trail. It looked freshly mowed. The trail goes straight into the wetlands along the bay.

The vegetation is thick out there. I looked around from the end of the trail and couldn't believe how close I was to civilization. I noticed fiddler crabs on the path (I'm glad I had on hiking boots). I also saw a hawk swoop down, but I didn't have my camera ready to take a photo. There are several side trails that expose hardwood pine areas. I took photos of some interesting flora I could not identify. It was a beautiful, peaceful day. A clear blue sky, 72 degrees, a very nice day.

I took a lot of pictures on the hike out to a plaque that memorializes the lady after whom the trail is named. It's posted on a large granite rock and mentions she spearheaded a grassroots effort to save this part of Tampa from land developers. She passed away in 1993 and didn't live to see this trail named in her honor.

DECEMBER

DECEMBER 1

Today would've been my sister's sixtieth birthday. Sadly she passed away from kidney disease in 1983. I'll always remember how much fun my twin brother and I had playing with her. Her name was Marylou. I called her Lu-Lu, and Tom called her Mary-Lu-Lu.

DECEMBER 2

Frank Cerabino of *The Palm Beach Post* is a serious journalist who does hard-hitting articles about state and local politics. He has quite a following, and his opinion is valued in the community.

In this morning's paper, his column took a slightly different turn. He wrote about me and the Florida Skunk Ape. He came upon *floridabigfoot.blogspot.com* while surfing the web and was intrigued by it. He called me on the phone and we spoke. He likes the videos and had all kinds of questions about tree-knocking and footprints.

In his column, Cerabino wrote: "Fasano walks through Florida swamps, woodlands and forests about three days a week in search of Bigfoot. It's more than a hobby with him. He has devoted countless hours to the hunt and posted YouTube videos of suspicious footprints and audio clips of animal howls. His website makes for enjoyable reading for anybody who has the inclination to imagine that the mythical Bigfoot creature lives in Florida."

He quoted me as saying, "Florida contains some of the wildest areas of remote, dense jungle and unexplored areas. I was very interested in exploring the universe and finding out why we are here. With all the oceans explored, now the great explorers must look inward to find mythical beasts."

DECEMBER 3

There was thick humidity last night. It hung over Tampa like a guilty conscience and wouldn't leave. I knew tonight was going to be off kilter.

I picked up a gay couple at the IHOP on South Dale Mabry. They wanted to go to Palm Harbor. A good ride. As we were going down Kennedy and approached Lois Avenue, I decided to turn right and go to the interstate. One guy said that was the wrong way to go, that if I went down Kennedy the lights would all be green, and it would be quicker. He was wrong, but tonight he was right. This guy kept complaining that Tampa was a tired city with not much nightlife. He wouldn't shut up. I finally asked him compared to what. He said Manhattan and South Beach. He said he hadn't been to

Miami since Versace's murder, and who knows Miami anymore since the Gucci store relocated?

Later I got this guy from the Howard Johnson's on South Dale Mabry, and he was sweating bullets and shaking. He said he wanted to go to a walk-in clinic. I told him that a "Doc in the Box" wasn't open at that hour. I took him to Tampa General. Next time he needs to take an ambulance. I hope he wasn't contagious.

The next fare complained that his bar pickup had her girlfriends with her, and they were "cock blocking." When we got to his apartment, he had no money. He thought he could write a check. My policy is no checks, but I took it anyway. I've been doing this for a long time, and I sensed no malice. He was just young and a goofball.

DECEMBER 4

I see a lot of accidents and often stay after to tell the police what I saw. On Halloween I was a primary witness to a bad accident with injuries at Kennedy and Howard. I've been a witness many times over the years, but nobody has ever contacted me about them.

Until today.

Someone was pounding on my door — not knocking but pounding with a key chain. When I opened the door, there was a woman from the Sheriff's Department who wanted to know if I was Tim Fasano.

I asked her what it was about, and she repeated in a harsh tone, "Are you Tim Fasano?"

"Who wants to know?"

She said if I continued to be evasive she would arrest me.

I told her who I was and asked what she wanted. She said I must've been in an accident and needed to go to court. I told her I'd never been in an accident in my life (a lie) and would like to know why she was at my front door and I'd appreciate it if she left. She said I needed to go to court, handed me a subpoena, and left.

DECEMBER 5

When I was taking passengers to the cruise ship from the airport, most of the downtown roads were blocked. I could see people in Nutcracker outfits and people wearing Santa hats. A Christmas parade was starting.

DECEMBER 6

Homicide detectives made an arrest in the murder of a Tampa cab driver. Devante Bell, 19, was charged with the death of Bay Cab driver John Dooley, who was found in his cab in the driveway of an abandoned house near Rowlett Park around 7:45 Sunday evening.

I risk my life as a taxi driver every day and have to worry about criminals like Devante who want to rob and kill.

DECEMBER 7

I'm sick, and so is my taxi. This flu bug is back, and every joint in my body hurts. My car was scheduled for service today. I also needed to have a new heater installed. It's getting cold now, and my customers will appreciate the heat. I brought the car in at 8 A.M. for what was going to be a three-hour job. They offered me a loaner cab, but as bad as I felt, I just wanted to go home. So I decided to wait — bad call. Somehow Steve messed up the fuel line, and the car began spilling fuel all over the place.

I was in the shop all day until they closed. Mostly I lay sleeping on the bench. Marjorie came in, and I thought she was going to say *there's no sleeping on the bench*. I'm sure she said something, but I was too out of it to hear her. Her boyfriend, Lester, came by with the Christmas trees for the office and asked me to help him unload them. When he saw what rough shape I was in, he said go back to sleep. I felt like shit. At the end of the day, nothing was fixed. Lester drove me home.

DECEMBER 8

This morning wasn't much better than yesterday. The office called and said the cab was ready. I went and got it, and when I was on my way to an airport call, smoke started billowing from underneath the hood and through the vents. I thought the thing was on fire. I took it back to the shop.

What gets me is all the money I lost because of this. I still don't have my car back. I'm going to go to bed and just try again tomorrow.

DECEMBER 9

The cab is running okay now, and this morning I picked up a fare at an addiction treatment center called DACCO Behavioral Health. That fare alone paid my lease for the day. I was feeling pretty good about myself and how I'm setting these calls up. One falls off. Another comes along. Success is when preparedness meets opportunity.

DECEMBER 10

Deputy sheriffs at the Port of Tampa are always harassing and browbeating cab drivers.

On weekends we commonly pick up tourists who want to go to one of the many cruise ships at the port. What usually happens is when we arrive there's a different procedure from the previous week. Today I arrived at the Carnival dock, and the deputies had the area coned off and wouldn't let me in. I waited to see if they'd remove any of the cones. They didn't. Other deputies were yelling at me to move. I swung around and approached again. This time they still wouldn't let me in, so I dropped my fare off at Hooters. She had a ton of luggage and was inconvenienced by all this.

DECEMBER 11

Working the hood at night isn't good for a cab driver. There's an overwhelming number of low fares, no-shows, laundromats, runners, and angry people — enough to make it unprofitable and annoying to the driver. You could work all night and not make a dime and be treated like shit the whole time.

That's why I seek out places where I'll meet positive people. So meet Mike. He comes from a hardworking immigrant family who owns a corner market just across the street from my hotel room. The Kwik Pik sells tons of lottery tickets, cigarettes, and beer. Swisher Sweets are a popular item. The selfie I took this morning shows Mike behind the counter with an exhausted taxi driver in front of him. Is my ashen face a sign of a life deferred? Is my reward another day of this? What's disappointing is I haven't been able to hike. I've been too busy putting in the hours of a West Virginia coal miner.

DECEMBER 12

The doctor said I could get a second opinion if I wanted one, but I needed to begin treatment now. He diagnosed me with advanced cellulitis, which is now poisoning my body and may have entered the bone of my lower right leg, which would mean immediate amputation.

It seems the flu I've had isn't the flu. It has everything to do with the red, swollen, and painful right leg of mine. It's an opportunistic infection. The word *cellulitis* means inflammation of the cells. It generally indicates an acute spreading infection. He said even amputation might not save my life. Whatever happened to a bedside manner?.

With no insurance, I have to pay for treatment out of my pocket. I can't afford what he's suggesting. When I told him I couldn't afford this, he became noticeably irritated. He seemed unable to comprehend that cab drivers have no insurance.

I don't know what to do. I don't know if I have it in me to even blog anymore. I need a leg, right? How can someone go this quickly? I'm sitting here shivering and sweating simultaneously even though it's a warm day. I'll post to my blog when I can. I've hit rock bottom.

DECEMBER 13

I've been receiving injectable and oral antibiotics. They seem to be having some effect. The doctor recommended that I be admitted to the hospital (only $10,000 a day). He kept saying he can't take responsibility for me. I guess he's afraid I'll get Morgan and Morgan and sue his ass. What's he done other than save my life? I haven't been working much, just resting and hoping for the day I can come back strong.

DECEMBER 14

This is very close now to the end of the line. The state of the business is such that our call count, which used to be as high as three thousand a day, is down to three or four hundred. Saturday, by the time Shoe came on, our phone system had been down for fourteen hours, and the company gave us no consideration on the lease.

I can't pay my lease, I can't pay my rent, I can't pay my phone bill, I can't pay my Internet bill, I can't pay any bill. I can't even afford a generic box of macaroni and a small can of cheap sauce to have some semblance of a dinner. One thing you find out when you're poor is you begin eating the starch diet.

I thought by not having much food to eat I might lose some weight. Not so on the starch diet. I'm at a point now where I'm going to have to give this up. It's been a good fourteen years. At least the first twelve were decent.

I'd be better off on the street, holding up a sign. That way if I collected a dollar, I wouldn't owe anyone any part of that dollar. It would be my dollar. I could put that dollar in the bank and at the end of the month I'd have thirty dollars, and that'd be more than what I've got in the bank right now. So I don't know why we still have hundreds and hundreds of cab drivers, all of them making the conscious decision to live in a state of grinding poverty, accepting it, and working sixteen hours a day, seven days a week, weekends and holidays, for the privilege of being dirt poor, *Tobacco Road* poor, *The Grapes of Wrath* poor.

DECEMBER 15

Syd, our shop foreman, was a dispatcher a few years back before taking some time off. One of the things he likes to do is go to Alaska to hunt big game.

In his office is a trophy of a moose head. Not too bad. They're enormous animals and not for the faint of heart to hunt. I've heard many first-time hunters are afraid to shoot one because they think shooting it will only make it angry. On the wall next to the mount are photos of the hunt. Alaska is a sportsman's paradise with hunting, fishing, and camping, unlike anything you'll find in Florida.

Our boss, Mr. Ryan Percy, is a deer hunter, but even he will go up to Alabama and Georgia to hunt. I like to camp and hike, so hunting doesn't interest me. I don't like killing animals. I like feeding and petting them.

DECEMBER 16

"It ain't about how hard you hit. It's about how hard you can get hit and keep moving forward."
— Rocky Balboa.

I've always believed it's the myths people create in the times they live that say more about them than what intellectuals say. Why? Because myths come from the heart and soul of people. Every civilization has striven to understand life and provide answers to explain the inexplicable cruelty of life.

The myth of Rocky Balboa is the belief that the common man put into an extraordinary situation can obtain greatness. The challenges we face in life aren't always about the outcome but about reaching down inside when having our spirit tested and for a brief moment exceeding beyond our grasp. After all, if your goals don't exceed your grasp what is heaven for?

I read the script of *Rocky Balboa* two years ago. It's more inspiring then the original. In the first movie, Rocky had everything to gain by fighting the heavyweight champion; now he has nothing to lose.

Penniless, his wife dead, his new girlfriend in danger of losing her halfway house unless she can come up with several hundred thousand dollars, Rocky doesn't know what to do and walks into a bar one night, and ESPN is on the TV. They're playing a computer version of what would happen if Rocky Balboa fought Mason Dixon (the current champ). The computer says Rocky would win. Then Dixon is interviewed and says the computer was racist and that he would kill Rocky. Everywhere he goes he keeps hearing about Dixon. One day in Circuit City he's looking at about forty images of himself, and he hears the bell ringing. Now he's ready to fight.

DECEMBER 17

My friend Roland was robbed last night. The news said police are seeking a fifty-to-sixty-year-old man who robbed a 7-Eleven on Gandy Boulevard with a sawed-off shotgun. The man went into the store with the gun and demanded money from Roland and got away with $40. When another employee came around the corner, the man quickly left. No customers were in the store at the time of the robbery. The man is described as white about 200 pounds with a medium build and salt-and-pepper hair. He left in a gray four-door 1990s model Toyota Avalon.

DECEMBER 18

Calvin Washington died. He was a cab driver in Tampa for over twenty years. Everyone knew Calvin. Many people today are sad.

Calvin was most famous for sleeping on the stands. The only picture I could find of him, of course, shows him sleeping in his cab. I knew Calvin well, and I'm sure he would laugh at me for posting this image to my blog. Many times, after being asleep for several hours, a taxi driver would check on him to see if he was okay.

Yesterday, on STAND 81 at Nebraska and Sligh, he was not okay. They found him dead. There was no indication of foul play. Calvin had many health issues consistent with a man his size. He was fifty-one years old.

Calvin grew up in Tampa. He played football for Hillsborough High as defensive end. He told me he loved to sack the quarterback. He was most happy about recovering a fumble in a crucial game against Plant High School back in the day of Plant's dominance.

A lot of people I know have died this year, which makes me understand the real meaning of *carpe diem*: seize each day as it comes. I remember when I was younger, I was going to grab life by the balls, but life grabbed mine instead.

DECEMBER 19

Today was one of the best outings I've had into a deep jungle area along the Dead River in Hillsborough County. I saw a tremendous amount of wildlife and evidence of large animal activity. I still need more time to get into this area and do an overnight and set up trail cams.

There was a large abundance of wildlife today. The importance of wildlife and water is that it's necessary for the existence of a large Bigfoot. Food is important, and eating plants and bark cannot sustain a massive primate.

I believe trail cams are the way to go. It doesn't seem likely I'll walk up to Bigfoot and take a video of him like Patterson did. He hit the lotto that day. I don't expect it ever to be repeated. The only thing Bigfoot field researchers can do is go out and put in the work. One day, one of us will get lucky. That you can count on.

DECEMBER 20

What a great Christmas dinner we had at Allied Cab! Mr. Ryan Percy has done this every year since he became the general manager. It's quite a gesture on his part, and I, for one, enjoy it. There's nothing that says he has to do it — he just does. The food was good, and I liked socializing with the staff and other drivers.

This year it was catered by Florence Green, a driver whose catering service did a fantastic job. There was turkey, ham, stuffing, green bean casserole, shrimp pasta, salad, fruit, rolls, and pumpkin pie.

From the *somebody up there likes me* category, I won the door prize. They said it was a gift certificate. It turned out to be a $250 Visa card. Maybe somebody up there does like me after all. I couldn't have known that from the last few years.

DECEMBER 21

I found a series of footprints of a primate along Cow House Creek (a tributary of the Hillsborough River) near Tampa. I have no way of casting prints at this point in my research career; however, I did get a good series of still shots. There were a total of three prints lined up toward the river bank. The water is rather nasty, but they need it to survive.

DECEMBER 22

A billboard on Kennedy Avenue asks an important question: WHO'S WAITING FOR YOU? Well, on this night, not a lot of people. Tampa was a ghost town. With all the people we took to the airport who went away for the holidays and people who're just laying low, not much was going on.

I tried my best. I drove up and down South Howard Avenue because of all the restaurants and bars, but there just wasn't any business. No big deal. New Year's Eve is days away: the Super Bowl of cab driving.

I did pick up an interesting character wearing hip hop garb. The entire conversation went like this: I'd talk and whatever I said, he had three responses: 1) "You know how it is." 2) "It's all good." 3) "True . . . True." Despite his limited verbal responses, he actually said more to me than most of my fares ever do.

I tried to see if I could create some business, so I went by a regular who usually will call early to go to her restaurant job; but because it was a warmer night, she rode her bike and was kind enough to pose for the camera, flipping me off as she made her getaway.

I did, however, return to Ballast Point for another fine sunrise. A pelican this time was willing to be my subject against a great Tampa skyline. It was very peaceful there.

DECEMBER 23

A newspaper article this morning was about how no president gets a fresh start after his first year on the job, but considering the size and scope of the problems President Obama inherited, 2010 could provide an opportunity to hit the reset button. After a long and acrimonious fight over health care reform, Obama will begin next year by signing a historic piece of social welfare legislation.

What I need in my life is a chance to hit my own reset

button, to move on from this quagmire that's gripped me like a bear trap for too long.

DECEMBER 24

Today is a special day for people all over the world. I have a huge feast planned with turkey, ham, pork, shrimp, mashed potatoes, salad, creamed spinach, and Uncle Ben's Rice.

I'll be alone this Christmas, but I did have a visitor. My good friend Sampson from Ethiopia dropped by to wish me a Merry Christmas. In Ethiopia he was a professional videographer, and he explained to me that movement is important for video. We discussed the videos I've been uploading to YouTube, and he gave me some advice on how to make them more engaging: angles, positioning, music, that sort of thing.

DECEMBER 25

The holiday season is a time to reflect on my blessings and imagine what's possible for my life.

All of us have gone through hard times. We just need to know there's a cosmic order that'll somehow be with us during it all. Merry Christmas to all and a Happy New Year!

DECEMBER 26

Last night I lit my Christmas candle, which I light only once a year. I backdrop it with the greeting cards I've received. I had only two this year, one from my special customer, Frank, and another from my sister-in-law, Sandy.

When I went to sleep, I dreamed that I was twenty-years-old again, and I could see my mother and father. The feeling of peace was overwhelming. They must be in a better place, but I'm not ready to join them. I have so much more to do, and projects springing up every day. I'm busy. This death thing doesn't interest me.

DECEMBER 27

I'm looking forward to the new year. Like most people, 2009 was a miserable year. It has left me broke, spiritually dead, destitute, and hungry. Soon I'll be dependent on other people to help me with some basic needs, things I don't bother with anymore — like food, clothing, housing, and grooming. Such is the way of depression.

DECEMBER 28

I was in Hollywood Video today, poking around in the CLEARANCE bin for a movie I saw a few years ago. It's called *Hell Cab*, also known as *Chicago Cab*. The movie was a flop, earning only $23,946 at the box office. Nevertheless, there're some big names in this rarely watched gem, including Laurie Metcalf, John Cusack, Gillian Anderson, and Julianne Moore. Paul Dillon plays the cab driver.

This movie is the ultimate "Taxi Cab Confessions." A cabbie starts his day on Christmas Eve, and everything that can go wrong does go wrong. The writer, Will Kern, is a playwright who wrote this story originally for the stage.

I suspect he's either driven a cab or consulted cab drivers about how screwed up many fares can be because of how realistic the film is. The drug runs and the people bringing their arguments into the cab and the guys telling women they love them only to have sex with them — it's all too real for someone to have imagined. Stuff happens to drivers nobody could make up, like the time I picked up a woman who'd just beaten up of her boyfriend after catching him turning gay tricks. When she got in my cab, all she had on was her bra. Clearly, she was a troubled person, and trouble for the fare means trouble for the driver, i.e., the less likely we are to get paid.

DECEMBER 29

This morning Marjorie told me she might fire me as

soon as tomorrow. Truth is I owe the company a tremendous amount of money. She said she didn't want to, but this may be the end if I can't fork over a grand to pay an outstanding lease. I'm screwed. Fine fucking chance I have of making that kind of money — even if it is New Year's Eve.

None of this is my fault. The economy has been horrific for the last two years. It's challenging to make high lease payments to your company, plus gas, and still be able to make money.

I've been struggling badly. On most days now, I wait about two hours to get a five-dollar fare. I can't make it on that. I put gas in the cab this morning with pennies and nickels.

The company relies on refugees from Third World countries who have a high degree of tolerance for poverty. They're willing to work sixteen-hour days, seven days a week, holidays and weekends for meager wages. They think they're rolling in clover, unaware of how bad their situation is.

I can't do what these guys do. I need someone to help me, but there's nobody in my life who can. I'll miss the old days of cab driving, the good times and good people who used to drive for a living.

When the economy ended up in the toilet, I had to move into a dive motel. I have to pay these people every week, or I move out. Simple as that. If I lose my job, I'm homeless.

My main concern is where to store my digital photography equipment, TV, stereo, and laptop. I'd like to hold on to that stuff. The rest of my stuff (books, clothes, and other collected items) I can throw away.

I don't know how to live on the streets. I do have a sleeping bag, and my sister-in-law sent me some lovely comforters. They'll come in handy. I have a backpack in which I can carry some gear around.

That's about it. The story of my life: in my fifties, and I end up on the streets.

DECEMBER 30

I do have my blogs and a successful YouTube channel. I got a check once from Google for advertisements. Perhaps, one of my blogs will become popular, and I will no longer be in dire straits.

I can go to the library to edit my blog. So there may be some long-term hope. There's a mission on Kennedy Boulevard where I can get a hot meal every day.

DECEMBER 31
Wish me luck.

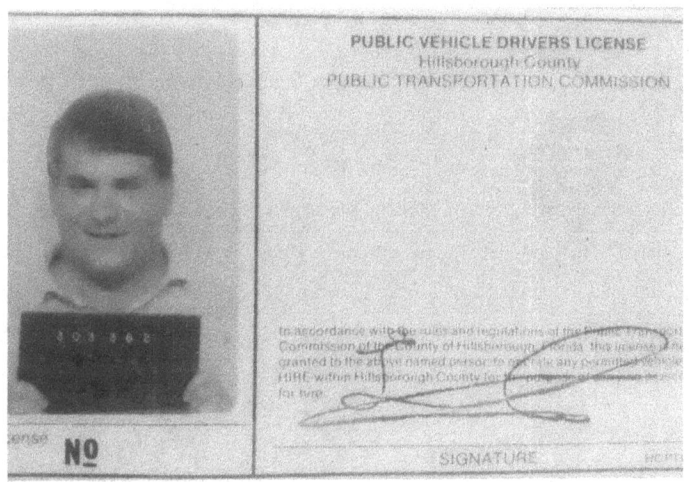

POSTSCRIPT: Tim eventually quit the cab business to drive for a rideshare company but was never able to pull himself out of poverty. He died of cardiac arrest in November, 2019.

www.ingramcontent.com/pod-product-compliance
Lightning Source LLC
Chambersburg PA
CBHW011255040426
42453CB00015B/2408